Matzo Balls
for Breakfast

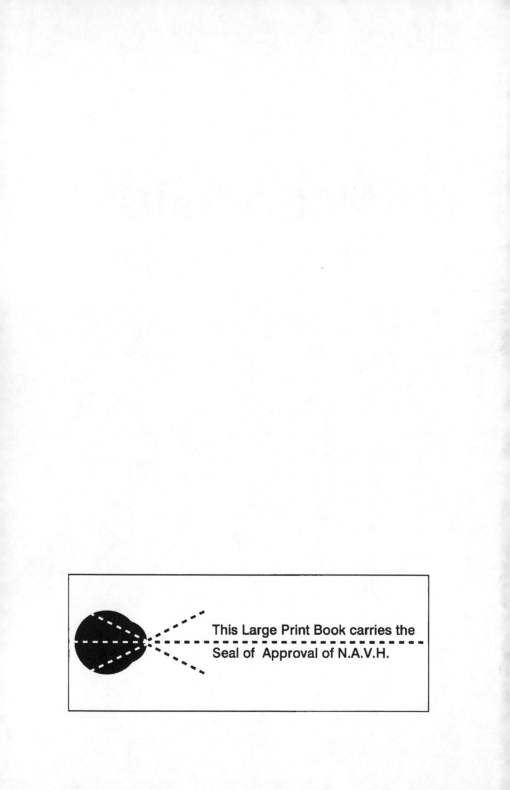

This Large Print Book carries the
Seal of Approval of N.A.V.H.

Matzo Balls for Breakfast

and Other Memories of Growing Up Jewish

Alan King
and Friends

Thorndike Press • Waterville, Maine

Published in 2005 by arrangement with Free Press,
an imprint of Simon & Schuster, Inc.

Thorndike Press® Large Print Nonfiction.

The tree indicium is a trademark of Thorndike Press.

The text of this Large Print edition is unabridged.
Other aspects of the book may vary from the original edition.

Set in 16 pt. Plantin by Minnie B. Raven.

Printed in the United States on permanent paper.

ISBN 0-7862-7320-8 (lg. print : hc : alk. paper)

Matzo Balls
for Breakfast

As the Founder/CEO of NAVH, the only national health agency solely devoted to those who, although not totally blind, have an eye disease which could lead to serious visual impairment, I am pleased to recognize Thorndike Press* as one of the leading publishers in the large print field.

Founded in 1954 in San Francisco to prepare large print textbooks for partially seeing children, NAVH became the pioneer and standard setting agency in the preparation of large type.

Today, those publishers who meet our standards carry the prestigious "Seal of Approval" indicating high quality large print. We are delighted that Thorndike Press is one of the publishers whose titles meet these standards. We are also pleased to recognize the significant contribution Thorndike Press is making in this important and growing field.

Lorraine H. Marchi, L.H.D.
Founder/CEO
NAVH

* Thorndike Press encompasses the following imprints: Thorndike, Wheeler, Walker and Large Print Press.

Contents

Part IV: My Defining Moment; or, Discovering the Essence of Being Jewish

Foreword

by Larry King

The show must go on.

That is what Alan King wanted. This idea that the show must go on is part and parcel of Alan King's essence; it's also a part of American Jewish tradition. Despite all kinds of adversity, we persist. We persist at making our children's lives better, at overcoming prejudice and anti-Semitism, at being true to our principles, but mostly we persist at keeping our optimistic spirit and unsinkable sense of humor.

Like you, I was greatly saddened by Alan King's passing in May 2004. I miss him terribly. But this sadness is tempered by the fact that my memory of him is strong, and stronger still because of this book. *Matzo Balls for Breakfast* started as a collection of memories, stories, anecdotes, and remembrances of the lives of prominent Jews about growing up Jewish. But it is now more than that: *Matzo Balls for Breakfast* is also a tribute to Alan King, who was not only one of the greatest Jewish comedians ever but also one of the greatest comedians period, and a heck of a nice guy, too. Alan lived a fulfilling and happy life. His fifty-seven-year marriage yielded three children and seven grandchildren. Alan starred on television shows and movies (twenty films!), and he wrote books. He joked with the queen of England, he hosted the Academy Awards, he was an emcee for John F. Kennedy's inaugural celebration. So when you shed a tear for Alan, be sure to smile, too. I will.

Alan King was a dedicated writer as well as a comedian. He was working on this book almost until the day he died, and it was virtually finished when he was taken from us.

Alan was as proud of his Jewish upbringing as anyone could be. His Judaism was as much a part of him as the air that he breathed. And so he would have wanted to see this book published. The show must go on.

PART I:

LIFE IN THE JEWISH FAMILY AND NEIGHBORHOOD

Mama and *tateh, bubbe* and *zaideh,* Aunt Sophie, the gang of kids down at the ball field, the waiters at the kosher resort in the Catskills — this is the cast of characters of the Jewish family and neighborhood . . . and they're all here. You expect the memories to be warm and fuzzy, and many of them are. But some have a pungency, a kind of sharp undertaste to them, like a bit of horseradish that got mixed in with the sweet *charoseth* at the Passover table. There are stories from Chicago and Brighton Beach and Miami Beach and L.A. and points farther afield, and so the background may vary a good deal — but in some very basic ways, the song remains the same. To me, it's like listening to new music and warming to hear echoes of old familiar themes in the chorus. Enjoy!

— Alan King

From Manhattan to Allentown to Washington, DC

Susan Stamberg

For fourteen years, Susan Stamberg has been the cohost of National Public Radio's *All Things Considered*. She is an Edward R. Murrow Award winner and a Broadcasting Hall of Fame member.

Growing up in Manhattan in the 1950s, I thought the whole world was Jewish. Well, *my* whole world was! Yes, my public school classes had a Despina Chilakis and a Diane Grimaldi. But mostly we were Levitt and Fortgang and Goldstein and company. Every weekend, my dad took us down to the Lower East Side for knishes at Schmulka Bernstein's (today it's Bernstein on Essex, a *glatt* kosher Chinese restaurant where the waiters wear little red silk yarmulkes with tassels). Or to Yonah Schimmel's. We were ethnic Jews more than observant ones. Still, I was sent to Temple Rodeph Sholem for confirmation classes. I found them most interesting. Until our teacher, Mr. Lear, decided to switch from Hebrew lessons to lessons in the rhumba. When I objected, I was called to the principal's office with my

17

mother. I said I was there for language, not fancy footwork (I was much too earnest a child, I see now). Either they invited me to leave school, or I parted in protest — I can't quite remember. My mother was mortified and, I suspect, a bit proud. So much for my formal Jewish education.

It wasn't until I married Louis Collins Stamberg of Allentown, Pennsylvania, that I realized the world included rhumba dancers who were *not* Jewish . . . not to mention people with two left feet, people who thought Jews had horns, people who were deeply immersed in very different faiths and beliefs. My husband, growing up, knew just how many Jews there were in Allentown. His family belonged to the Reform temple and the Jewish country club. The Stambergs of Allentown were self-consciously Jewish. They knew they were in the minority, had neighbors who didn't like living near Jews, and practiced traditions that defined them as Jews in a town that didn't reflect those traditions back to them. Allentown was not New York.

Neither is Washington, DC, where I've spent my adult life. Yonah Schimmel? Knishes? Stuffed derma? We don't have a single decent deli in our nation's capital! You can't buy a rye bread with any zest to it, let alone find pastrami that makes your mouth water just ordering it. Sometimes I wish the whole world *was* Jewish. Usually on weekends. At lunchtime.

⌐◦⋰⊙⋱◦⌐

Brighton Beach, the Music, and Mom

Neil Sedaka

Although a classically trained composer, Neil Sedaka has written multiple number one pop hits, including "Breaking Up Is Hard to Do," "Laughter in the Rain," and "Love Will Keep Us Together," which won a Grammy for Record of the Year in 1975.

I was born and raised in Brighton Beach, which was a unique section of Brooklyn. In the 1940s, it was a lower- to middle-class Jewish neighborhood where everyone looked the same and talked the same, families spoke Yiddish at home, and by having little contact with other neighborhoods, I thought the whole world was Jewish. I spent glorious days at the Brighton Beach Baths, where I saw great performers, like the Barry Sisters, singing in Yiddish. On family picnics, we would all sing *"Shen Vi Di Lavone"* and

19

"Beltz Mein Shtetele, Beltz" on the bus.

My first performance as a singer occurred at my bar mitzvah when I was thirteen at Temple Beth El in Manhattan Beach. I attended Hebrew school five days a week after regular school. Soon I could read and write Hebrew so fluently that I was able to teach my sister Ronnie as well. But the thing I enjoyed most was singing the Haftorah. The day of my bar mitzvah, when it was my turn to sing, I got up at the podium, and my stage fright vanished. By the end of the Haftorah, there wasn't a dry eye in the house. My voice, I had discovered, was an instrument with wide-ranging possibilities. Afterward, the cantors took my mother aside and suggested that she think seriously about her son becoming a cantor. She was flattered. "But I'm afraid Neil has other plans," she said. "He's getting a Ph.D. in music to be a teacher."

I attended Lincoln High School on Ocean Parkway. I got my training in the Catskill Mountains, playing in a band at the Esther Manor Hotel. I accompanied such greats at Totie Fields, Billy Eckstein, and Hines, Hines and Dad. I was studying to be a concert pianist at the Juilliard School of Music. I had to wait until my mother left the house to go shopping, so I could write my rock-and-roll songs. She was horrified at my neglecting Chopin and Bach. But . . . Mom got used to it.

***

> There is a quiet humor in Yiddish and a gratitude for every day of life, every crumb of success, each encounter of love.
> — Isaac Bashevis Singer

***

A Blessing for Yakov Robinson

Alan Dershowitz

Alan Dershowitz has represented such high-profile defendants as Claus von Bulow and O.J. Simpson. He has been a professor at Harvard Law School for more than a quarter of a century. He is also the author of more than a dozen books, including two best sellers about Jewish life and culture, *The Vanishing American Jew* (1997) and *Chutzpah* (1991).

I grew up on the same street on which Jackie Mason and Sandy Koufax lived. It was a thrill for me watching Koufax pitch, even though he was quite wild when the Dodgers were still in Brooklyn (I stopped caring when they moved to L.A.). I also got a thrill from listening to Jackie Mason's comedy (he was pretty wild, too). But my biggest thrill as a Jew growing up in Brooklyn was seeing Jackie Robinson become the first African-American to break into baseball. Of course all of my buddies aspired to become Brooklyn Dodgers. We even adopted nick-names appropriate to the sport. I was "Red" — an unlikely name considering the current color of what little hair I have left. Because I had a good arm, I was going to re-place Billy Cox at third base. Sure, it was a fantasy; deep down I knew I'd never make it into the majors. What I really wanted to be was the president of the United States.

The day Jackie Robinson walked onto the field in 1947 with that beautiful Dodger uniform, I realized for the first time that fantasies could come true — that as a Jew, I could achieve any goal to which I aspired. If Jackie Robinson could play for the Brooklyn Dodgers, Avi Dershowitz (that was my name in Brooklyn) could be-come president. A law professor at Har-vard? That was another thing. I couldn't even get into Harvard, so my imagination did not stretch *that* far.

Jackie Robinson was our hero, our role model, our dream. Before his first at bat we wanted our rabbi (an old European Jew who never heard of baseball) to give him a special blessing (a *mishabeirach*), but of course the rabbi would never knowingly waste the blessing on such frivolous activity as baseball. So we created the name Yakov Gnovtbaben, which is Jackie Robinson in Hebrew, his last name broken into the three words "rob," "in," and "son." The rabbi made the blessing, Jackie got a hit, and we believed in God — at least for the moment.

Four years later, when Bobby Thompson of the hated Giants hit his infamous home run just before a major Jewish holiday, there was a significant abandonment of faith. Brooklyn in the 1940s and 1950s was a place where hope ran supreme and optimism knew no bounds. The Depression was over. We'd won the war. Parents had jobs. And the streets were our playground. We could play anywhere, do anything, without fear. A young man like me was judged not on his grades (which sucked), nor on his good looks (use your imagination), but on his sense of humor and his prowess at stickball and spitball. I was pretty good at those.

My conduct in school was deplorable. I once actually got an F in "plays well with others" (some things never change). My mother was my first defense attorney, though she went to college for only one month and left when the Depression hit. She was called to school so often that my friends thought she worked there. One day the principal called her in and told her about a particularly horrible thing I'd done (making a dummy of myself and throwing it off the roof, pretending that I had jumped). The principal shook his finger at my mother and said, "What are you going to do with him?" My mother banged the table and said, "I'm going to keep him. That's what I'm going to do with him." And she did.

I'm very nostalgic about Brooklyn. My gang of eight (seven other guys I grew up with, went to school with, and went to camp with) still get together two or three times a year to tell Brooklyn stories. Some of them are even true.

A Lost Soul

Bernie Siegel

A pediatric and general surgeon, Bernie Siegel is also the author of *Love, Medicine, and Miracles*, a book about the mind–body connection in healing.

"Growing up Jewish"? My first thought is that the subtitle of this book is an oxymoron. Because Jewish parents have a way of keeping you from ever feeling you have grown up and matured.

I was born at the Jewish Hospital in Brooklyn, New York, in 1932. Due to medical problems my mother experienced, which made a cesarean section too risky, and complications of labor, I was born an ugly duckling. Our family album shows my carriage covered with blankets so no one could see me. If anyone removed the blanket, my mother tells me, I was also wrapped in kerchiefs to hide my head. Fortunately I had what the ugly duckling didn't have — a Jewish grandmother, who massaged me and "pushed everything back where it belonged," to quote my mom.

I lived most of my childhood years at 1453 East Third Street between Avenue M and Avenue N. The house still looks as it did during those years. I went to P.S. 226, which was a long walk over trolley tracks and busy streets every morning, but my parents and grandparents trusted me and even gave me the responsibility of getting my sister there safely, too.

Our synagogue was around the corner on Avenue N. My grandparents were Orthodox Jews who kept a kosher household and came to this country to escape persecution in Russia. My grandfather was a Hebrew teacher and told me stories about how the Cossacks would ride him down and attack him with their sabers if they found him out at night. I will never forget caring for a man at Bellevue Hospital, while I was in medical school, who had a deep V-shaped cleft in his skull. He told me the Cossacks had inflicted it upon him when he was a child in Russia and out in the street as they rode by. He had been left for dead but managed to survive. After seeing him, I understood what my grandfather went through.

My grandfather was my Hebrew teacher. We sat in the basement every evening and I was his student. I never attended Hebrew school at our synagogue. I think I had an unusual childhood with parents, grandparents, and teachers who appreciated how bright I was, and so I skipped two grades, and I was comfortable with the God my grandfather represented to me.

We lived in a house with one bathroom and six people, but I can never recall any problems about it being accessible. I do remember locking myself in when I had a fight with another kid on the block and knew I was in for trouble. My sister was very devilish, and my mother used to put a harness on her and tie her to the drainpipe so other kids could walk by our house without being assaulted.

Our street was like family. We all sat outside on hot nights and played punchball, johnny-on-a-pony, or stoopball. I remember once going out of the country without a passport. When I came back, I told the agent I had forgotten my passport.

"Where were you born?"

"In Brooklyn."

"What's a stoop?"

"The front steps of a house."

"Okay, you can go through."

I laughed, and we talked about the questions he had on file to determine if people were telling the truth about where they were from.

The real point of my writing is to tell

you about my fall from grace. As I said, we were all family and my closest friend was Carmine Birsamatto. He was Catholic, and I was in awe of his living room with Jesus looking down from the artificial fireplace and how beautiful and spiritual it was at Christmastime. I stayed home from school with Carmine on Catholic holidays and he stayed home with me on Jewish holidays. It was fun for both of us. Our parents didn't know about our routine.

One morning I was at Carmine's for breakfast and his mother served something that tasted delicious. I asked what it was so I could tell my folks about it.

"It's called bacon."

"Thank you, Mrs. Birsamatto."

When I got home I immediately sought out my parents and grandparents to tell them about this great meal I had just had. When I mentioned bacon, I thought my grandparents were going to pass out. I could see that heaven was no longer an option for me. Years later I realized I could still be saved when I saw the words, "Everything you remember I forget and everything you forget I remember," and read in the Yom Kippur service that God forgives us for our sins against God. My parents and grandparents, as well as my wife and I, celebrate Hanukkah — but Santa Claus, who has no religion assigned to him, also shows up with gifts for our five children and eight grandchildren every year.

For my bar mitzvah, my grandfather wrote an eight-page speech, which I memorized. I have no memory now of what I said because it was his sermon, not mine. I could see his face filled with pride as I delivered this long sermon from the pulpit just as we had rehearsed it in our basement.

When I graduated from high school, I went off to Colgate University, on scholarship, in upstate New York, where Judaism simply didn't exist. I wasn't discriminated against in any significant ways except not to be a member of any fraternity. However, not having the opportunity to practice my religion affected my relationship to Judaism. The first seder ever held at Colgate happened while I was there. (Today Colgate has a Jewish Center, and our family has given a significant donation to help create it.) I graduated in 1953 with honors and from there went to Cornell Medical School, again with a New York State scholarship, back in good old New York City. I was married by then, and my wife taught kindergarten out in East

Meadow, Long Island.

I decided not to remain in New York after riding the subway for four years and seeing what the crowding and noise did to people. It didn't feel like family anymore. I have run several New York Marathons and I love the spirit of the city on that day when every race, religion, and nationality is out on the street cheering and nourishing you spiritually and physically.

Today as a surgeon I know we are all one family, and I like to show a slide when I lecture and ask people to tell me the race, religion, nationality, and sex of the person in the picture. They can't because it is a photograph of our insides, and we are all the same inside. I think it has been an advantage to be a Jew, because I have studied other religions to help my patients, and I see how many of them create feelings of guilt and punishment. Jews can talk to God and bargain with Him, like Tevye in *Fiddler on the Roof,* and I have the same faith in Him that Abraham and Jesus had, despite what they were asked to do.

Maimonides, the Jewish physician and philosopher, is a great teacher. He said, "If people took as good care of themselves as they do their animals they would suffer fewer illnesses." I'll say amen to that. He also said that disease is a loss of health. So I always ask people, if they lose their car keys, does it mean God wants them to walk home? If they laugh, I say, "Then if you lose your health, go look for it. God is not punishing you or taking it away."

I asked a rabbi why rabbis always answered questions with questions. He said it was to make people think, and when he didn't know the answer he would tell a story. He went on to say one can always find a blessing in the curse and that the Bible interprets the word *"tov"* as "good," relating to everything God created except man.

"So man is no good?"

The rabbi said, "The word 'good' has lost its meaning. A better translation of *'tov'* is 'complete.' Man is not complete, and all the things we experience that help to complete us, even when painful or life-threatening, can become our blessings. As my mother said when I came home with problems: It was meant to be. God is redirecting you. Something good will come of this."

"You're right. I did a lot of conversing with God as a teenager because my mom didn't seem to get it, but I learned with time she was right."

Someday I hope we recognize that our differences are for recognition and not destruction, and love becomes the weapon of choice, and we all become complete. As Golda Meir said, "When we love our children more than we hate our enemies, wars will cease." Then the Cains and Abels will apologize, and we will be family again.

Today I enjoy the wisdom of Talmud and kabbalah and am less concerned with the rituals than with their meaning and what I can learn about living from them. I think fundamentalists of all religions cause problems because words become their God and not deeds or acting like God. For me, love is God and God is love.

Incidentally, I am on the board of directors of heaven as an outside consultant. One day I asked God why He didn't make a perfect world free of problems and difficulties.

He said, "A perfect world is a magic trick and not creation. So live and learn and understand that by giving you a choice your acts become meaningful." He also said that when I give a report to the board to end with the words, "The beginning."

"Why should I do that when I am finished?"

"Because life is a series of beginnings

and we must use change and loss, learn from them, and move on just as we do when we finish school and have a commencement."

> The most remarkable thing about my mother is that for thirty years she served the family nothing but leftovers. The original meal has never been found.
>
> — Calvin Trillin

My Alteh Zaideh

Monty Hall

Monty Hall is the cocreator of *Let's Make a Deal* and starred as its emcee for twenty-three years.

I was brought up in Winnipeg during the Depression years. My father, mother, younger brother, and I were forced to move into my grandfather's home. There we joined six of my mother's brothers and sisters and my grandfather's parents — my two great-grandparents. Fourteen of us in one house with one bathroom! From this crowded house came a close bonding of family, respect for the older generations, and terror for your bladder.

One of my duties at the age of eight was to accompany my great-grandfather to shul on Saturday morning. He was in his mid-eighties and rather frail (incidentally, he lived to be ninety-one — never exercised, smoked unfiltered cigarettes, and ate everything with a half inch of shmaltz slathered over it), and so he needed assistance for the long walk. After services we started the trek homeward. My *alteh zaideh,* knowing of my desire to eat a quick lunch and go off to the movies, spoke *"Gai shoyn, gai shoyn!"* Go already. He would release my hand and I'd race home to wolf down my lunch. As the three uncles and I started off to the movies, there he was slowly, slowly making his way home.

Ten years later I would leave our apartment and walk to my grandfather's home to accompany him to shul. He was in his sixties but was blind as a result of diabetes. We walked with our hands clasped together in his coat pocket and talked of everything from college studies to hockey games. Ours was a close and wonderful relationship. This truly was being Jewish by osmosis.

Anthony Weiner

Representative Anthony Weiner was elected to the New York City Council in 1991, making him, at age twenty-seven, its youngest member ever. He has represented Queens and Brooklyn in the United States House of Representatives since 1999.

I'd love the arrival of the seltzer man. The perpetually S-shaped guy with Popeye arms would bring a wooden case with the old, heavy glass squirt bottles and take our empties. He had Hoffman's sodas in long-necked returnable bottles on the truck, too, but my family never got that. But sometimes, if life was particularly good in Brooklyn, we did get a bottle of Fox's U-Bet. Egg creams, anyone?

> I do not recall a Jewish home without a book on the table.
> — Elie Wiesel

My Favorite Deli

Jay Winik

Jay Winik is a historian and the author of the best-selling book, *April 1865: The Month That Saved America.*

One of my first vivid recollections of growing up Jewish has to do with my bar mitzvah. At the age of ten, I decided that I loved sports more than I cared about religion, let alone my Jewish education. Football, baseball, boxing — that was what I wanted to do. I skipped Hebrew school so often that I basically quit; it was a fait accompli that I imposed upon my parents. A few years later, however, I still wanted a bar mitzvah — to have the ceremony, to become a "man," to have the party. I got Hebrew tapes from which I learned what I was supposed to say and do — or so I thought.

It was a grueling chore, curled up in my bed, night after night for months, memorizing, chanting, over and over again. Eventually I learned my part, and just in the nick of time: about a day or so before my actual ceremony. (By the way, this wonderful work habit would repeat itself for years right up until I was an undergraduate at Yale, cramming for Shakespeare and history courses, invariably the night before the final. Only later, when I started writing books, did I finally become enormously disciplined.) With some trepidation and a healthy dose of excitement, I was finally ready.

On the anointed day, a heavy snowstorm blanketed New England, including my hometown of New Haven, Connecticut, but that did not stop the ceremony. I passed, which is to say that I read my lines adequately and with no mistakes. But there was one thing that I neglected. Although I knew my text, I had forgotten other aspects of the ceremony. Actually, it was quite comedic. When the rabbi and everyone else on the biman turned around, I stood proudly, still facing the guests. Whoops. When the glass of wine was set before me, I instinctively — heaven knows why — picked it up and slugged it down like I was chugging a Coke. Whoops again.

The other thing I tend to associate with growing up Jewish, and I admit this at the risk of sounding totally unenlightened or like a Philistine (or both), is the food. As a kid, Saturdays were the days we'd go to the local deli in New Haven. It was called Chuck's. A meal at Chuck's was a fixed routine: Eat at the same table, usually with the same people (my family and boyhood friends), see the same crowd every week ("Hey, how ya doin'?"), eat the same pickles (the best), and the same food, usually thickly piled corned beef and melted cheese on rye. Going to Chuck's was a sort of comforting ritual, repeated so often that it became part and parcel of growing up. To be sure, there were the holidays, the family vacations, and the sports. There was the onset of adolescence, with all that entailed. But there was always Chuck's.

Many years later, after I had grown up, moved to Washington, DC, and married, I returned to New Haven and stopped by Chuck's to have a meal. A stroll down memory lane, as it were. Alas, Chuck's had closed. It was a neatly decorated Vietnamese restaurant, or something like that. Next door was a Laundromat. Down the block was a trendy Italian restaurant, awash in potted ferns, and on the corner was a large Staples. The block seemed so antiseptic . . . quiet . . . changed . . . different. It felt like the passing of an era.

These days, I live in upscale environs of suburban Washington, DC. The restaurants my wife and I eat at are fancy American or Italian, or chic Greek, or finely rendered French. We have a small son, Nathaniel, with bright blue eyes and a keen sense of joy and wonder, who will grow up knowing "the right places" and "the right people." He'll know the inside of the White House and the Supreme Court. He'll know fine art galleries, good clothes, tony schools — his likely pre-school at a local synagogue takes four-year-olds on field trips to the Kennedy Center and the ABC News offices of *Nightline* — and Four Seasons resorts. He'll know Santa Barbara and Manhattan, London and Paris. He'll probably be spoiled to death. But will he ever know a place like Chuck's?

Encouragement When You Need It Most

Bill Macy

Best known for his role as Walter Findlay in the television series *Maude,* Bill Macy portrayed the character Dr. Isaac Sobel in the 1999 film *Analyze This,* with Robert De Niro and Billy Crystal. He has appeared on such television shows as *The Love Boat, St. Elsewhere, Seinfeld, Chicago Hope,* and *NYPD Blue.*

In New York City in 1968, I was in a production of George Tabori's *The Cannibals*, a play about the Holocaust. At the end of the play, the cast walked through the audience to our deaths. My mother had a seat on the aisle, and as I passed her, she leaned over and whispered to me, "Excellent."

Everyone should have a Jewish mother.

> Pessimism is a luxury that a Jew can never allow himself.
> — Golda Meir

My Son . . . Not a Doctor

Joel S. Kaplan

As president of B'nai B'rith, one of the largest and oldest Jewish organizations worldwide, Joel S. Kaplan is a tireless advocate of Jewish and humanitarian causes.

My sister and I grew up in Brooklyn. We were children of the fifties, and our parents had all of the preconceptions about the paths that their progeny should follow. My parents worked hard — my family had very little money — and their primary goal, particularly my mother's, was to see to it that both my sister and I got an education that would enable us to make our way through life.

After graduating Brooklyn College, I attended New York University Law School, and to this day I recall with startling clarity leaving the hall after the conclusion of graduation ceremonies and walking down the aisle with my new wife, Joan, my parents, my in-laws, and my sister-in-law, very proudly contemplating my future. When I was approximately halfway out of the auditorium, I felt a tug upon my sleeve, and there was my mother, all five feet zero inches, looking up at me and indicating that I should slow down and let the rest of the family leave, she wanted to talk to me. Once the family was twenty or thirty feet ahead of us, my mother looked at me and said, "Son, if you would like, I will put you through medical school." Can any more be said about a Jewish mother? Like an enormously high percentage of her peers, my mother felt that becoming a doctor would be the epitome not only of my life but also of hers. I must confess, however, she did learn to make do with a lawyer for a son.

My "Hasidic" Father
Ruchama King Feuerman

Ruchama King Feuerman is the author of *Seven Blessings*, a novel about a woman's search for a soul mate in Jerusalem.

I remember getting myself ready for school in the morning, and the first thing I'd see was my father, in our living room, sitting at the far end of our couch, praying from a siddur, his phylacteries wrapped around his head and arm. The siddur was in English. He'd started getting involved in religion when he was in his thirties, and he never got the hang of Hebrew.

When I finished in the bathroom and peered over the railing, I could see him unwrapping the phylacteries, at which point our cat, Wilbur, would grab hold of the black straps, and there'd be a little tug-of-war between the two. I never gave the image much thought, except on those days when he was sick.

Unfortunately, any day of the year my father could check himself into a hospital, if he wanted to, and be admitted for some medical problem. It made me feel off-kilter when my father wasn't sitting there, on the yellow couch, hunched over and concentrating on the words.

My father started out with zero knowledge of Judaism. My siblings and I, enrolled at the local Hebrew academy, were supposed to fill in the gaps. When I was in third grade, my father asked me at what sections was he supposed to bow down during the silent devotion prayer. I took a stab: "Whenever it says, 'Blessed art thou,' bend your knees and bow down." He followed what I told him until his rabbi came over and told him four bows would suffice instead of the nineteen he'd been doing.

My father both admired rabbis and suspected them. He was convinced the whole kashruth industry was a scam dreamed up by rabbis to make money, and only in later years, having studied the actual laws, did he keep strictly kosher. When a certain rabbi would get up and speak, my father would tell me later, "Nice talk, but that man loves the sound of his own voice." And yet he was almost slavishly devoted to his rabbi. When it was time to set up the chairs for an event at the synagogue, he'd be the only one doing it, every single time, and the only one folding the chairs away. The same with putting up the sukkah.

People thought he was the janitor. The rabbi's wisdoms, both biblical and off-the-cuff-life insights, filled our Shabbat table conversations.

Mostly he taught me never to ignore another human being, which, when I was a teenager, could be embarrassing. He'd walk into a bank, see a grotesque-looking lady, and spread out his arms. "Darling, you look like a million bucks!" I'd cringe and turn away. This was the South in the seventies, where one could say such things. Outside I said, "Dad, how do you know that lady?" He spread out his hands, as if to say, *Beats me.* He once saw an old Chinese woman in traditional garb wandering through the streets, obviously lost, not knowing a word of English. He said, "This one's mine," and took her home and through hand motions and other charades tried to get a family member or name out of her. She was terrified. When her brother finally tracked her down, he found the two of them singing "Fiddler on the Roof," the only English my father managed to conjure out of the old woman. This mitzvah, good deed, was his, all right. He was ambitious to do a kindness.

When I was living in Israel and came home summers, I was always amazed at the people he collected, hanging out in the den: Ellwood, the carpenter; Miriam, a teenager whose mother had died; Dan, who needed tutoring in math; Sylvia, an opera singer; and Bennett, the three-year-old kid next door. This unlikely crew enjoyed each other's company, with my father's joke cracking and counseling serving as a backdrop. There was something actually cool happening in my father's den. Even I, his skeptical daughter, couldn't deny that.

Once I asked him, "Dad, what would you do if you found ten thousand dollars in the middle of the street?"

He looked uncomfortable. He said, "I don't know."

"What do you mean you don't know? You'd return it, right?"

He said, "I'd like to think so, but I honestly can't tell you what I'd do."

I was furious at him. This was my pious father? The one who'd inspired me to take religion seriously, to make Israel my home? And then I read a tale of a rebbe who posed the same dilemma to three students. The first answered, "I'd return the money." "You're too glib," said the rebbe.

The second said, "I'd keep it." "You're a thief," said the rebbe.

The third said, "I'd want to keep the money, and I'd pray to God with all my being, to give me the strength to resist." "You're a Hasid," said the rebbe.

My father, despite or perhaps because of his contradictions, is a Hasid.

> It took me a long time to learn that you don't have to be a rabbi to be a Jew.
> — Kirk Douglas

Aunts, Uncles, and Grandmothers

Carol Bruce

An original Broadway cast member of Irving Berlin's *Louisiana Purchase*, Carol Bruce was a regular radio performer in the 1940s, sang with live bands, and did comedy and variety shows on television for many years.

My first story about growing up Jewish relates to my aunt Sophie. I think every family ought to have an Aunt Sophie. She had a strong Russian-Jewish accent. And her voice! Her voice was so rough, it sounded like someone was tearing a rag into two pieces.

One year, my aunt Sophie came to visit me in my small apartment in New York City. My career was on hold and my finances were in a slump and I was distressed and depressed.

My dear aunt Sophie told me, "Carol, darling, money doesn't bring you happiness, but it certainly calms your nerves!"

Aunt Sophie was full of such wise advice. When others in my family bemoaned the past, thinking about what could've happened or what should've been, Aunt Sophie would say, "Children, vat vas, vas."

Another memory that comes to mind is of Passover at Uncle Ben's. Uncle Ben was a very observant Jew; he held every protocol affiliated with the seder. This meant he read the Haggadah in its entirety. Every word!

One year, I must have been about ten or eleven years old at the time, I remember the sinking feeling of acute boredom. When it came time for the youngest child to ask the Four Questions, the youngest member of our party diligently asked the most memorable question, "Why is this night different from all other nights?"

I quipped, "Because we never get to eat!"

I can still remember how my uncle's

stare curdled my blood.

On the weekends, I used to go out to the Bronx to visit my grandmother. We would sit in the kitchen on Friday nights while she made chicken soup. I'd sit on the stool in the kitchen and strum songs on my ukulele. We'd sing together in Yiddish. Maybe it's just those nights that led me to choose singing as a part of my career.

One night I took my grandmother to a Chinese restaurant, which, of course, wasn't kosher. I ordered pork and told her it was chicken.

"Oh, it's delicious!" she exclaimed. And then, in Yiddish, "Carol, darling, you light up my life."

❦

Yiddishkeit

Iris Rainer Dart

Iris Rainer Dart is the author of eight novels, including the bestseller *Beaches*, which was made into a film starring Bette Midler.

I was born in Pittsburgh, Pennsylvania, to immigrant Jewish parents who survived the pogroms of Russia, and in my household, more Yiddish was spoken than English. I heard so much Yiddish that as a child I didn't know which language was which. When I was four years old, the gentile children next door to our tiny house invited me for dinner. When their mother was serving the meal, she asked me what part of the chicken I wanted, and I said, "the *fleegle.*"

I remember very clearly the perplexed look the woman gave me, which I thought meant that there probably weren't enough *fleegles* to go around, so I hastily assured her, "That's okay. I'll be just as happy with a *poulkie.*" She still didn't know what I meant and told me, "Just point to it, dear!"

My Yiddishkeit was simply a part of who I was. One reason was that my *bubbe* Chaike, my mother's mother, lived with us for a while and she never spoke any English at all. Chaike was a great influence in my life. I realize it more and more the older I get.

In the early part of this century, when my grandfather left Russia with the two eldest of his nine children, Chaike was left at home to raise and support the remaining seven in any way she could. So she dug a hole in the dirt floor of the two-room house, slid a still into the hole, and by night made moonshine whiskey, which she sold to the Cossacks.

Then she stashed the money, which she later used to buy passage to America for the rest of the children. Chaike taught me that Jewish women can do anything. One of the things Chaike refused to do was speak English. She said she didn't have to. She had nine children, they had nine spouses, there were twenty-two grandchildren. We all understood her Yiddish. So who else was she going to speak to? A stranger, maybe?

Chaike's daughter Rose, my adorable mother, was the quintessential Jewish mother. Though she came over from Russia when she was twelve, she always spoke ninety percent Yiddish and spoke English with a pronounced accent. She taught my nephew Larry to talk, and he was the only child in nursery school who, when asked, "What does the doggy say?" replied, "Bow Vow Vow."

With a twinkle in her eye and a Goldwynesque confusion about words, she would keep us in stitches.

Once, my sister's cat, Puff, had an altercation with a raccoon, and when my mother heard about it, she called and asked, "So . . . did you hear vat happened to Puffy? It's so terrible. He vas bit by a kangaroo."

Once, when my mother and I returned to Pittsburgh from a trip, my brother picked us up at the airport. As we headed for the parking lot, my brother spotted the local mortician waiting for a cab. "Oh, hi, Mr. Blank," my brother said. "May I offer you a ride home?"

"Oy vey," my mother said under her breath. She was so superstitious that she couldn't bear the thought of the under-taker sitting in the same car with her. But Mr. Blank accepted the offer. All the way home, my mother averted her eyes to avoid the man who had buried every loved one she'd ever lost. When we finally arrived at his house, and he was about to get out of the car, by way of bidding good-bye to him, my mother said, "Listen, Mr. Blank, I'll make you a deal. Maybe since ve took you, you vouldn't take us."

In Pittsburgh there were two big cleaning companies that cleaned draperies. One was called Werner's and the other was called Vernor's. After my mother sent out our living room drapes and they didn't come back, my sister said, "Ma, where did you send the drapes?"

And my mother said, "Verner's."

51

"Is that Werner's?" my sister asked.

"Yeah," my mother answered.

"Or Vernor's?"

"Also yeah," my mother replied. The drapes finally came back.

She had a particularly Jewish way of mothering her children by teaching us that the only way to make it through this life was to have a sense of humor. There was the time I saw her writing a check to the synagogue for two hundred dollars. My father was a social worker in a settlement house. We had very little money, and two hundred dollars was a big donation. I asked her why.

She told me with a twinkle in her eye. "Last year I gave a hundred dollars. But I told the rabbi, 'Listen, Rabbi. Next year I'll live and be well, I'll make it two hundred.' So my luck, I lived."

Seven years after my father died, when my mother was sixty-five, she remet her high school boyfriend. In high school, she had referred to this five-foot-two guy as a short cut; at sixty-five she described him as "a handsome sheik." When he proposed, she was hoping we'd give her a shower and wanted us to buy her a white nightgown. "Why do you want a white nightgown?" my cousin asked. "You're not a virgin anymore." She said, "Listen, after so many years, maybe I am one again."

Now *that's* a sense of humor.

⚜

Brighton Beach

Gloria Dubov Miklowitz

Gloria Dubov Miklowitz has written more than sixty-five books for children and young adults. Her most recent books are *The Enemy Has a Face, Secrets in the House of Delgado,* and *Masada: The Last Fortress.*

I grew up in Brighton Beach, New York. From the first days at school I didn't know a child who wasn't Jewish. I once went to my junior high on a Jewish holiday. There were four children in class.

The boardwalk: We used to play cops and robbers in the pavilions. On the beach, in winter, snow covered the sand. The only prints were those of seagulls. One night, after a day of snow, I begged my big brother to take my sister and me to the boardwalk on our sled. He pulled us through a thick pillow of virgin snow in a silence interrupted only by a brush of

53

wind. The next day the snow had turned to slush.

Brighton Beach sounds: The elevated train passing regularly on one side of our building, the surf pounding on the other side. The screech of seabirds. Fireworks exploding into the night sky, seen from the apartment rooftop every summer week.

Summer: School's out. The days are hot and sunny. By nine in the morning we fly out of the apartment in bathing suits to spend the day at the beach. "Please, Mom, bring us lunch. Please, Mom. We're starving by two o'clock." By August we are so sunburned that it hurts to don the starched yellow dress mother has ironed, so stiff it stands bodiless on the bed.

Yom Kippur: Walking, walking, talking with friends, dry-mouthed, hungry. At home, still honoring the fast, the sisters and brothers tempt me by waving bread in front of my face.

Elementary school: Scared of walking down the alley to P.S. 100, the smell of damp woolens in the wardrobe. Going to the Tuxedo Theater on Saturdays for cartoons. Going to Coney Island and getting sick from too much cotton candy and too many rides that go round and round. And Nathan's hot dogs! Yum!

High school: Typing out a story in the *Lincoln Log* office, the fun of being part of a newspaper, falling in love for the first time.

Returning to Brighton almost fifty years later: It's the same, but different. Jewish Russians live there now, and the neighborhood is still clean and well cared for. Mothers walk the boardwalk, pushing their babies in strollers. Old folk sit on the benches, looking out to the sand and the sea, hearing the trains pass over the avenue, hearing the surf break against the shore.

There was no anti-Semitism when I was growing up in Kenosha. There was a Jewishness among everybody — Italians, Poles, Lithuanians — all their families came struggling out of Europe.
— Irving Wallace

Bubbe*'s Basement*

Faye Moskowitz

Faye Moskowitz is the author of *Her Face in the Mirror: Jewish Women on*

Mothers and Daughters; *And the Bridge Is Love: Life Stories*; and *A Leak in the Heart: Tales from a Woman's Life*. She is chair of the English Department at George Washington University.

Who could doubt that our *bubbe* was a magician? We had only to watch as she turned a simple ball of thread into lacy snowflakes with a wave of her tiny crochet hook. And the cookie jar that seemed to have no bottom, forever brimming with nut-studded *mandel* bread: Wasn't that something out of a fairy tale? Surely sleight-of-hand made it appear whenever we did. How to explain *Bubbe*'s challah, the sticky mix of flour, eggs, leaven, and water turning into a pliable dough when she kneaded it under her capable fingers. What else but legerdemain accounted for that round, yeasty pillow rising, rising, in its greased bowl, slowly lifting the clean dish towel with which she bedecked it? *Bubbe*'s ice box called to mind a miniature car at the circus, but instead of colorful clowns, out tumbled an endless parade of apples, oranges, plums, and apricots. We cousins popped in and out of our grandparents' Detroit home in the 1930s and '40s, always certain of something delicious on the porcelain-topped table in *Bubbe*'s cramped little kitchen, always certain of the magic words, *"Ess, ess, mein kind."*

But *Bubbe* practiced her most serious alchemy in the dark, musty cellar of her home on Hazelwood. I remember calling for her sometimes when I came to visit, listening for her voice reaching me from far down in the netherworld that dwelt beneath the sunny two-flat. Years later, when I read Poe's "The Cask of Amontillado," I thought of descending the rickety wooden stairs to look for *Bubbe*, remembered how I shivered, even in summer, in the cool, damp of weeping cement walls and ceilings so low I could imagine spiders skittering down silvery threads to catch in my hair.

Like any character on a journey in a folktale, I had to undergo many trials before I could reach my *bubbe*. First I had to make my way through the fruit shed, lined with shelves on which jars of secret potions bubbled. Some were filled with glistening dill pickles and green tomatoes put up in the fall, announcing themselves by their briny, garlicky scent. Others contained preserved sweet Michigan cherries that we ate in winter with a pillow of sour cream, all the while worrying about swallowing those pits our mothers constantly warned us about, the very ones that could cause appendicitis or worse. *Zaideh* made the heavy sweet wine we drank on holidays, crushing the dusky Concord blues into a fragrant juice that fermented in wooden barrels before he poured it into bottles he placed next to the pickle jars. He must have been a magician, too, because, at Pesach seders, after our parents allowed us to drink a bit of that grape juice, we all fell asleep under the table or on *Bubbe*'s bed as if we were under a spell. The next morning when we awoke, mysteriously in our own beds, each of us might have been Sleeping Beauty, aroused from a hundred years' slumber.

A fierce ogre guarded the next room of *Bubbe*'s basement. Of course I knew it was only the coal furnace, just like the one we had at home, but it was so much more fun to imagine it a scary creature with a fiery red mouth. Beneath the round belly of the furnace, *Zaideh* shook down the "clinkehs" with a lever like the crank on a Model T. The fierce grinding of metal against metal could have been the great ogre shouting, "Fee-Fi-Fo-Fum." At least I convinced myself it was.

Bubbe's laundry room, redolent of bluing, bleach, and Fels Naptha soap, came next. I gingerly made my way around her Maytag washer with the rubbery wringer lips that could swallow my arm right up to my armpit if I got too close. I called out, *"Bubbe,* I'm coming," just so those skeletons dangling limply from her clotheslines wouldn't get any ideas. No one could convince me they were merely *Zaideh*'s union suits, smelling faintly of mildew as they waited to dry in the cellar's winter chill.

And then finally, there was *Bubbe,* her familiar turban slipping rakishly down her forehead, her hair covered as pious women were instructed to do. *Bubbe* stood stirring a witch's brew in a large earthenware crock. One by one she dropped in the ingredients: peeled magenta-colored beets with their tails cut off, sugar, garlic, crumbling bay leaves, tiny pellets of allspice, and a handful of kosher salt. In a few days the resulting fermented *rossel* would suffuse the entire house with a smell so awful we kids would giggle with embarrassment and pretend not to notice. And there again was magic. For on Pesach, when we all gathered for the first seder, my aunts marched carefully out of *Bubbe*'s kitchen carrying flat soup plates of rosy sweet and sour *rossel borscht,* all the more delicious and precious for its once-a-year appearance. Perhaps *Bubbe*'s *rossel borscht* was her most magical trick of all, for half a century later, I can still conjure up the taste of that fragrant ruby nectar as if I had sipped it from my spoon only yesterday.

<hr/>

At Reuben's After the Shabbat Service

Alan Oppenheimer

Alan Oppenheimer is an actor who has been on such television series as *The Six Million Dollar Man*; *Murder, She Wrote*; and *Murphy Brown*. He has also been the voice of many animated characters, including Vanity in *The Smurfs*, Skeletor in *He-Man and the Masters of the Universe*, and the King of Gummadon in Disney's *Adventures of the Gummi Bears*.

Growing up in Manhattan, my aunt and uncle, who became surrogate parents (replacing my father, who died when I was nine), liked my sister and me to attend Temple Emanu-El with them for Friday services at five p.m. I would sit there twitching and couldn't wait for the benediction so we could kiss each other with a *"Goot Shabbos"* and get the hell out. Then we'd walk down the six blocks to Reuben's restaurant for a wonderful dinner with my aunt and uncle, Edie and Lester. This was 1944, and with World War II on, Mr. Reuben always had a long table of maybe twenty servicemen; one night the USO would send over the army, and the next the navy. Mr. Reuben gave them dinner and drinks, and my uncle, a veteran of World War I, would always send to the table a few pitchers of beer with his love and a thank-you for their serving their country as he had done twenty-five years earlier. As a young "man" of fourteen, I thought it marvelous to be dining and drinking with "men" a few years older than I, and also, I believe it was the perfect benediction to the Emanu-El service.

Everybody ought to have a Lower East Side in their life.
— Irving Berlin

Rocky Dale

Steve Bronstein

Steve Bronstein is the executive producer of Court TV's *Hollywood at*

Large, a weekly series that explores crime and justice in popular culture.

My grandparents fled Russia so they could escape living in a hut surrounded by anti-Semites whose idea of fun was a good pogrom. So, where did their first-generation American children — my parents — take me to live every summer? To a community of decaying huts surrounded by anti-Semites whose idea of fun was taunting us to go back to Russia, where we could be surrounded by anti-Semites whose idea of fun was a good pogrom.

It was a bungalow colony. That's where my parents took us each summer. Four rows of about eight ramshackle wooden shacks apiece nestled in the woods, with outdoor showers, a dirt tennis court with more holes than a golf course, a social hall where a common activity was dodging the wasps that made their homes in the rafters, and a cedar lake where our community of 130 or so Jews blithely coexisted with bacteria that probably don't have names yet. Every summer, Abe Glick, the resident doctor, gave us kids shots before a season of swimming in that lake. What was he giving us shots for? Tetanus? Malaria? I don't know, and we didn't care.

I never heard of a gentile going to a bungalow colony. Bungalow colonies were a New York Jewish phenomenon. You can still find the remains of some of them today scattered throughout the Catskills. Although most of the colonies have gone the way of chicken fat shmeared on rye bread — my grandmother's favorite snack — some of the colonies have been reborn as summer communities for New York Hasids. They are like summer camp for families.

Ours was called Rocky Dale Lodge. An hour into the farmland and tiny towns surrounding Philadelphia, two hours from New York, the nearest small city to Rocky Dale was named Quakertown — you're right, not a lot of Jews there. But our group of thirty-plus Jewish families came back religiously, year after year until the early 1970s, to spend the summer in the country.

For my mom it was a vacation from housework; the cramped three-room bungalow with its antique gas stove we lit with a match, the yellowed linoleum floor, and the weathered wooden planks of our porch was not worth more than a cursory once-over with a sponge and a mop. My mother's usual attention to cleaning was replaced by the clink of mah-jongg tiles. For my dad, Rocky Dale was a retreat from work and a place to spend his two weeks of vacation. Most of the fathers came up to the place once a week during the week and for the weekends. And for me, my brother, and my sister, it was a welcome (and cheaper) alternative to summer camp. Who wanted the forced discipline of counselors and a camp's rigid schedule when we could do whatever we wanted from the moment the sun woke us up in the morning till the crickets and fire-flies put us to sleep at night? We had the love and security of our family, plus almost every bungalow had a family with a kid our age. Swimming, reading, tennis, baseball, hikes, rock climbing, campfires. Nights in the social hall playing cards or basketball, while the big kids would take out the old phonograph and spin their new records. It's where I first heard Jimi Hendrix, Crosby, Stills & Nash, and Blood, Sweat & Tears.

There were two places my family wor-shipped each week at Rocky Dale. Friday nights we had services in the social hall. Although I'd guess it was mainly a way for the parents to say kaddish if they had a de-parted one's anniversary to remember, it was us kids who led the service. The years of Hebrew school were put to use for something other than our bar mitzvahs. Me, the son of a Jewish showbiz ham, I loved performing the *Yigdal*. And for all of us, the incentive to sit through the service was a Hershey bar with almonds handed out by old Julia Stern at the end.

But our other weekly place of worship was the drive-in. My brother, sister, and I would wait with our noses pressed against the screen door of our porch for Dad to come up from the city. That usually would mean a night out in Quakertown for soft ice cream at Dairy Queen, stale popcorn at the snack bar, and movies, movies, movies. Double or triple features. Bob Hope, Doris Day, Tony Curtis, Elvis Presley. Frank Sinatra as *Tony Rome*, Dean Martin as *Matt Helm*, *Godzilla* starring as himself. Even *The Godfather*. I saw them and loved them all at the drive-in.

Would I be a TV producer today without Rocky Dale? Probably not. I reveled in the laughs, thrills, and romance of the movies at the drive-in. I marveled at the revolutionary new sounds in music coming out of the big kids' phonograph at the social hall. I barreled through piles of books — Freud, Steinbeck, the collected works of

Jules Verne, H. G. Wells, and Ray Bradbury — and piles of comic books. And, with a writer's obsessiveness, one summer I devoted three hours each morning to sitting in front of my new typewriter and writing my opus — a take-off (as if it weren't one already) of *Get Smart*. I still have the rejection note from *Mad* magazine (the watermark on the stationery is the face of Alfred E. Neuman). That letter was as much of a reward to me — the budding twelve-year-old auteur — as if I had actually gotten my amateur little story accepted.

Around the campfires I developed my storytelling talents further. Most kids in the flickering light of the fire tell tales of the boogeyman. At Rocky Dale, we made up stories about "the Jew haters." They, we imagined, were the residents of the wooded roads and hidden huts surrounding our little Jewish enclave. Many a mailbox in the area did carry the name of a solid German-American family, and every once in a while a car filled with raucous teenagers would drive by the entrance to our camp and shout anti-Semitic slurs. In the nightmare light of the campfire, we took our neighbors a step beyond. We debated whose bungalow would be attacked first if the Jew-haters rampaged through Rocky Dale. We delighted in paralyzing Mickey Gelfand with fear as we detailed how the Jew-haters would skewer each member of his family. I loved to drag my stories out in a low, lulling voice — gory detail after gory detail — until Mickey was leaning in real close to hear and I'd scream out the punch line. We all loved to see him jump.

And then there were the shows. We were way off the Borscht Belt beat, so the parents put on their own productions on the rotting stage of the social hall: broad, boisterous, and I suspect more than slightly drunken skits and plays all spoofing life at Rocky Dale. Isabelle Biron, the resident pianist, banged the latest Broadway songs on the out-of-tune piano while the adults sang parodies, detailing maybe who had gained a little too much weight, or whose dog relieved itself inconveniently, or who could use a wardrobe update. It was all off-color fun. The parents did a cleaned-up dress rehearsal for the kids after services on Friday nights, but only I was allowed to see the actual productions. It doesn't hurt to have your father as the director, and someone sober had to turn the cue cards. I loved being around the excitement, the hilarity, the fun. And you wonder why I went into show business.

It's been more than thirty years since Rocky Dale closed. The bungalows have all been torn down, but the place still exists in the hearts of all the families who went there. My best and truest friends remain the same ones I had around those camp-fires. And we all agree that if we could grant our kids one gift, it would be a summer back at Rocky Dale Lodge.

***

Growing Up Jewish in Chicago

Jan Schakowsky

Jan Schakowsky represents the Ninth Congressional District of Illinois.

I grew up in Chicago's West Rogers Park neighborhood in the '50s, so, of course, I'm Jewish. Everyone was — well, everyone except Gretchen across the street and Ginny two doors away, and I felt sort of sorry for them, because everyone else was Jewish. I learned later that Gretchen was Lutheran and Ginny was Catholic, but those fine distinctions meant nothing to me. One was either Jewish or not-Jewish, a Jew or a goy. My cousin Fred was married forever to Virginia, a wonderful woman, and until she died she was the shiksa, no offense intended, although if she ever said anything remotely foolish, the eyes would roll and I knew what that meant. "The shiksa, you can only expect so much" — a *"goyisher kop"* — a gentile brain.

We all went to the neighborhood public school, which was virtually empty on each and every Jewish holiday. We pored over the *Weekly Reader* and fretted over Sputnik and vowed to be better at science, though I already knew it would never be up to me to put a "man" in space. The Russians didn't threaten us only in space; we would regularly have "air raid drills," during which we went into the hall, sat on the floor, buried our heads in our knees, and silently prayed that they wouldn't bomb Rogers School.

Speaking of prayer, we studied for our Constitution test in eighth grade, memorizing the Bill of Rights and discussing our Founding Fathers' great ideas like "separation of church and state." I understood better then, why, in my house, it was considered bad for the Jews when the words "under God" were added to the Pledge of Allegiance some years earlier. At first, when my class recited the pledge each morning, I would mouth those two words rather than speak them. That may have been my first act of civic protest.

I went to Hebrew school twice a week after regular school, and Sunday school where, naturally, God was mentioned quite a bit. Temple Menorah, a Reform synagogue, was not far from my house. It was one of dozens of Reform, Conservative, and a few Orthodox synagogues along California Avenue. For a while, they seemed to spring up overnight. Every time a few people got mad at the rabbi, they'd start their own congregation, hire a rabbi, and build a building. Every Saturday of my twelfth and thirteenth years was spent in one of them, though my memories of the services are much dimmer than my memories of the bar and bat mitzvah parties, including my own, and dancing the jitterbug with the boys.

Every Sunday we went to visit my mother's parents in the "old neighborhood" in the house where my mother grew up. Most of the time I liked to go because my grandfather, who was a fruit and vegetable peddler, kept his wagon and his horse, Teddy, in the barn — now the garage — behind the house. I loved being in that barn — the smell, the feel of Teddy. My grandmother had bottles of Pepsi in the pantry and she would make homemade french fries and Jewish delicacies like *tagelach*. She was a regular reader of the *Forvitz*, the Yiddish edition of the *Forward* newspaper, and was convinced that anyone who had his or her picture in the *Forvitz* was Jewish, including, of course, John F. Kennedy. My parents, particularly my mother, who was completely fluent, and grandparents conversed mainly in Yiddish, a secret language that I never mastered, except for key words and phrases. I learned bits and pieces about their life in Russia but, regretfully, not much. I am inexplicably proud of being a first-generation American.

Summers were sweet. When school was out, we packed up and went to our house in Michigan City, Indiana, right on the beach of Lake Michigan. It was an enclave for Jewish Chicagoans to escape the unrelenting heat of summer in the city and the polio epidemic of the fifties. My cousin Carrie, exactly my age, and her family were there, too, and we knew everyone in every house up and down the beach. Two summers, Carrie and I went to Camp Herzl, a co-ed Zionist camp in Wisconsin. There we played games that reenacted the formation of the State of Israel, swam in the lake, tormented our counselors, chanted the lengthy Hebrew prayer after every kosher meal, and had a wonderful time. When we returned to Michigan City, we insisted on the prayer after meals and insisted that the whole family sit at the table until we were finished. I loved going to Omaha, too, where there was a small Jewish community with lots of cute boys my age and a Jewish country club with a good pool.

At age twenty, I married a nice Jewish boy who had gone to the neighboring high school. We had two children who went to Hebrew school and Sunday school and had a bar and bat mitzvah. After an amicable divorce, I married a goy who discovered, at age fifty-two, that his great-grandfather was Jewish. Yes, Sol Bergman, the merchant, was Jewish. *Nu?* My husband is inexplicably proud of being part Jewish. In fact, I've never seen anyone, with the possible exception of Democratic candidates for president, more delighted by having discovered his Jewish heritage. I've noticed that since then, as best he can, he sprinkles his conversation with Yiddishisms, often slapping his head and whining convincingly, *"Oy vey!"*

My Judaism remained mostly mindless well into adulthood until I became an elected official, and the community made me understand that, like it or not, I was now a Jewish leader. I liked it. And I was deeply grateful, for the first time, to Mrs. Karlin, my Hebrew school teacher, who made me learn all the prayers that I can now belt out with the best of them.

> I'm just a nice Jewish girl from New York. Going back through my life now, the Jewish family feeling stands proud and strong, and at least I can say I am glad I sprang from that. I would not trade those roots — that identity.
> — Lauren Bacall

Diaspora in Miami Beach

Thane Rosenbaum

Thane Rosenbaum is the author of *The Golems of Gotham*, *Second-Hand Smoke*, and *Elijah Visible: Stories*.

Miami Beach, where I grew up in the late 1960s, and throughout most of the 1970s,

was a curious mixture of Jewish displace-
ment and possibility. Almost everyone I
knew was Jewish. There were all those
grandparents who had made aliyah to South
Florida, exiled from the Northeast, like
Moses — an army of walkers and canes —
making their exodus to Mt. Sinai, not the
mountain but the hospital on Biscayne Bay.
And there was an assortment of small-time
Jewish mobsters — loan sharks, bookies,
bagmen, and numbers runners — circumcised men of the Meyer Lansky's tribe,
goons who had only recently been kicked
out of Havana. And finally, there were the
Holocaust survivors. My parents were included in this bunch. These were the people
with the accents and the nightmares, the
dreams that couldn't be shared, analyzed, or
comprehended. They were refugees taking
refuge from their memories, blinding themselves with Miami's reliably potent sun from
the images that had already been seared into
their heads and branded on their arms. Perhaps they could simply burn it all away, or at
least tan over it. South Florida was the an-
tithesis of where they had come from and
what they had seen. The cloud cover was always tropical, not diabolical, the result of
low-lying moisture, not the ashen rainfall of
Jewish death. The black skies of Poland had

given way to the cloudless blue horizons of South Florida, and yet despite all the clear visibility, the mind of the refugee was still clouded up with the landscape of millions of unmarked Jewish graves and all that Jewish loss and abandonment. And no amount of pinochle or jai alai or the dog tracks provided enough of a distraction. Staring out onto the ocean, they awaited the oncoming smoke, doubling back, trailing those who thought they had gotten away. It would inevitably find them. No sunny backdrop, no deep-sea hideaways, could ever make them safe.

My kids are now so assimilated that they don't have what I had. I feel bad about that. I think that's a shame.
— Joel Grey

PART II:

A JEW IN A
NON-JEWISH WORLD

Anyone growing up Jewish eventually has to come to this realization: I'm different, somehow; I'm not quite like the rest of the world. If you grow up in a close-knit, nurturing Jewish family, within an enveloping Jewish neighborhood, it might take a while before that fact hits you. For the ones who grew up in the sole Jewish family amid a sea of gentiles, that knowledge is there almost from birth.

While being in a minority is always a part of the Jewish experience, what varies tremendously is how each Jewish boy or girl experiences the non-Jewish world. It's been the stuff of high comedy — as well as the darkest tragedy of our age, the Holocaust. Fortunately for American Jews, there's been far more comedy than tragedy in our dealings with the non-Jewish world, as this part of my collection shows.

— Alan King

Ed Asner

Ed Asner played Lou Grant on *The Mary Tyler Moore Show* and then became the star of his own series, *Lou Grant.* Among his other credits are roles in *Roots* and *Rich Man, Poor Man.* He also served as the national president of the Screen Actors Guild.

My young nephew, Harry, lived in Carbondale, Illinois — not a mecca for Jews. Walking home from the first day of first grade, Harry was in the company of another first-grader from the 'hood. In the course of the conversation, Harry happened to mention that he was Jewish and asked his companion what he was. He replied he was a Christian. Harry pondered this for a moment and then said, "Oh, are there many of you?"

❧

Baseball Was Our Religion

Murray Olderman

For thirty-five years, sports columnist and cartoonist Murray Olderman appeared in 750 daily newspapers, as well as in *Sports Illustrated, The Saturday Evening Post, The Sporting News,* and *Inside Sports.* He was voted into the National Sportswriters Hall of Fame in 1993.

Baseball was the game that Americanized us in Spring Valley, a small shtetl upstate from New York City and west of the Hudson River. Our village, en route to the Catskills and the Borscht Circuit, had its own kosher hotels and summer bungalows. The main colony of Jews was clustered on a hill that popped up east of Main Street, which was the demarcation line between us and the goyim.

We were all immigrant families from the ghettoes of Russia and Poland, Galicia and Latvia, and one anomaly three doors away, the Nordhausers from Germany. My father and mother were from the Ukraine. The only gentiles on Lake Street were Pete Hamilton and his family, who served a utilitarian function. They turned the lights on and off for *Shabbos* in this very Orthodox commune, particularly in our house. The young rabbi, Joseph Soloveitchik, was our tenant.

Across the street, with a broad vista west

over the valley toward the Ramapo Mountains beyond Suffern, was an empty lot where we nurtured our love of the ultimate American pastime. It was a rectangle, had rocks and weeds and clumps of grass and sloped away on one side, but it was our ball field. I hit grounders by the hour to my brother Dudie (for David), a natural infielder, and we played pickup games. We couldn't afford a regulation baseball, so we used a dime rocket (a cheap baseball purchased at Woolworth's or the five-and-dime, generally for about ten cents), and when the cover frazzled and finally fell off, we wrapped it with black friction tape and played on.

A couple of streets above us on First Avenue was a legitimate baseball diamond, the Eagle Grounds, where the big guys played in a twilight league, and we'd sneak onto the infield during batting practice to snag ground balls. We even sneaked out of shul to play one-a-catch, a tailored-down version of the game. Baseball was our religion.

Twenty-five miles to the southeast was the Valhalla of sports, Yankee Stadium, and we read about the legendary New York Yankees of Babe Ruth and Lou Gehrig, Tony Lazzeri, and Bill Dickey in the *Daily*

News, which cost only three cents, two cents if you got it in the city.

But my team was the Detroit Tigers, who were pennant winners in 1934–35; their starting lineup, embedded in my memory to this day, most importantly featured Hank Greenberg on first base. There had been Jewish players in the majors before, starting with Andy Cohen, who played second base briefly for the New York Giants in the late 1920s. And Buddy Myer of the Washington Senators won the American League batting championship in 1935. But none matched the greatness of Hank Greenberg, the premier home run slugger of his time.

So at the age of thirteen, I saved up enough money collecting silver foil from chewing gum, cigarettes, and other wrappers, rolling them into tight balls, and selling them to the local junk man, to make a pilgrimage, via the Rockland Bus from Spring Valley into the city and subway trains to the Bronx, to see the Yankees vs. the Tigers. I splurged $1.10 on a grandstand seat. Before the game, I ran down the aisles to the edge of the dugout for a close-up look at big leaguers, right down to the moles on their necks. Unfortunately, Greenberg wasn't among them. He had fractured his wrist and missed most of that '36 season.

When the ushers shooed me away, I started mounting the steps to the grandstand area and abruptly spotted this giant of a man with slicked-back dark hair in a reserved seat ($1.65). Completely out of character because I was painfully shy, I stopped and blurted, "Are you Hank Greenberg?" I was sure it was.

He barely looked at me and curtly said, "No." I slunk away. And went on with my life.

Ultimately reconciled to the realization I would never be able to hit a curve ball, I became in time a sports writer and cartoonist. In 1971, I came face-to-face with Hank Greenberg again. A celebrity tennis event called the Dewar's Cup was held that August at the Concord Hotel in the Catskills. A publicity man named Nat Fields lured me there to chase down some columns among luminaries such as Hall of Fame quarterback Otto Graham, baseball immortal Satchel Paige, and basketball's fiery Rick Barry. Rocky Graziano was supposed to be there, too, but the colorful ex–middleweight champ turned TV personality was a no-show. To fill out the field, Nat asked me to take Rocky's slot.

As luck would have it, I reached the finals, spurning a furtive offer of a case of scotch if I would throw the semifinal match against Ron Ziegler, then press secretary to President Richard Nixon. It would make better copy if Ziegler reached the championship round against — you guessed it — Hank Greenberg.

Pancho Gonzalez, then tennis pro at the Concord, was our ball boy. Hank beat me in a one-set match, six to two. It still made *The New York Times*. We subsequently became friendly-but-serious tennis adversaries at other special events and at his Beverly Hills Tennis Club when I was in Los Angeles, right up until a couple of years before he died in 1986. I never mentioned to Hank how I first encountered him fifty years earlier.

<hr />

Persecution

Neil Simon

Neil Simon's plays include *The Odd Couple*, *Barefoot in the Park*, and *The Sunshine Boys*. He was awarded the Pulitzer Prize in 1991 for *Lost in Yonkers*.

I didn't find out I was Jewish until I was fourteen. My parents wanted to save money on a bar mitzvah. From that point on I was chased from block to block by the Irish, the Italians, and the Germans. On Halloween, I was usually hit with a woman's stocking filled with wet white powder, which was eventually used in World War II. I went to a junior high school on Long Island, where I was the only Jewish person. They let me live because I was a good softball player.

When we moved to Phoenix, I was one of only five Jewish kids in elementary and high school. There was a lot of anti-Semitism against me and my sisters. In study hall kids used to pitch pennies at me, which would hit my desk and make a large clatter. It was called "pitching pennies at the Jew," and it was very hurtful.

— Steven Spielberg

Gerald Stern

Gerald Stern is a National Book Award winner and a National Endowment for the Arts grantee, whose books include *This Time: New and Selected Poems*, *Bread Without Sugar: Poems*, and *Lucky Life*.

In the early thirties, in a ridiculous attempt at partial assimilation, we moved from the old Jewish quarter in Pittsburgh, the Hill District, an absolute replica, with its cobblestone streets, tiny shops, and synagogues, of some Eastern European corner, to a goyish suburb of neat ugly houses and a woods full of black locusts and half-grown maples. We had a new car every other year, two peach trees, and a kitchenette, of which my mother was very proud. I was the only Jew in the local public school, and I got beat up more or less daily, or at least insulted and ridiculed.

My father, the youngest of nine, was born in a shtetl maybe fifty miles north of Kiev, and since he came to America in 1905 at the age of eight, he had no accent and bought completely into the American myth of cleanliness and equality. He adored animals, but since my mother, a traditionalist, was terrified of anything that crawled, flied, barked, or roared, we kept no animals, though for a short while she relented and we had a silly nervous little canary named Dicky.

My father and I were taking a walk one evening — I remember our street was called Fallowfield Avenue — when we came across a woman walking her dog, the poor thing proud, erect, its mouth open, its tail high, alert for anything. My father fell all over the beast, petting him (her), roughing him up, half dancing with him, almost kissing him. The dog was overwhelmed with pleasure and returned the favors. It was a love match made in dog heaven. The mistress, the owner, for her part was also pleased that someone would love her dog that much and stopped to take out a cigarette, which she would soon redden with her delicate lips. My father anyhow was in his late thirties at the time, a fine suit, a mustache, certainly a beautiful fedora, as handsome as they came. "He loves people," she said about her dog, "unless they're Jews. He can't stand Jews."

My father probably said nothing. I listened, and absorbed. Father Coughlin was already wound up, and Hitler, in some far-away land, was making good headway. We moved away three or four years later, partly because my sister had died, age nine, and partly to rejoin, to deassimilate. But whatever the meanness and stupidity of that vile lady, her dog, maybe a spitz-Eskimo, maybe an Airedale, favorite dogs of the time, had more sense and, in spite of her, kissed to death and loved forever one dear Jew, who walked away tightly holding the hand of his young son.

If you ever forget you're a Jew, a gentile will remind you.
— Bernard Malamud

What Are You?

Carole L. Glickfeld

Carole L. Glickfeld's novel, *Swimming Toward the Ocean*, traces the lives and loves of a Jewish immigrant couple. Her collection of stories, *Useful Gifts*, was awarded the Flannery O'Connor Award for Short Fiction.

Nowadays, when I meet someone in Seattle, the someone says, What do you do? And I say, I'm a writer. But when I was growing up in the Inwood section of Manhattan — at that time with enclaves of Jews, Italians, and Irish — you'd get asked the question, What are you? I'm Jewish, I'd say. What are you?

As a kid, I never thought about how I got Jewish. I was. I never thought about what it meant to *be* Jewish. I was. Just as I never thought about what it meant to be deaf, which my parents were. I, my brother, and sister could hear, but my parents could not. We "spoke" to them in sign language. The sign for "Jewish" is made by stroking your chin, as if stroking a beard, a rabbinical one, perhaps. You stroke your chin even if you're talking about a female someone or a male someone who is way, way too young even to have a hint of a beard.

My grandfather Abe — my mother's father — had a beard. He also had a house in Brooklyn with a walnut tree in the backyard. Unable to practice Judaism freely in the Ukraine, he had the courage to bring his wife and three children to the *goldeneh medina:* America, the golden country. He didn't speak English; he spoke only Yiddish. One of my great regrets is that I never learned to speak Yiddish with him. I communicated with my grandfather in ways akin to those he used with his deaf daughter, my mother.

Although some of our relatives spoke "Jewish," Jewish in my immediate family was unspoken. We ate kosher, we fasted on Yom Kippur, we bought clothes in Jewish-owned wholesale factories where my father had "connections." My public school, P.S. 152, emptied out for Jewish holidays. I went to my Brownie troop in a synagogue on Nagle Avenue. At the Y, I learned to dance the hora. My parents belonged to HAD, the Hebrew Association for the Deaf. Being Jewish meant being influenced not only by Judaism but also by Jewish culture, which osmosed through the pores.

Unspoken, too, was the envy I felt for goyish ways. I couldn't go to White Castle (which I imagined as hamburger heaven). I would never look like the movie star Jane Powell, blonde and pert with upturned nose. I would never be able to get my fist to meet a Spaldeen in punchball (non-Jewish girls seemed born athletic). I would never climb trees.

At the top of my neighborhood park, Fort Tryon, was the Cloisters, a reconstructed twelfth-century abbey with trea-

sures purchased by John D. Rockefeller Jr.
Down below, on the playground, my
mother congregated with her deaf friends
while I stood in a bathing suit under the
fountains of the wading pool. Sopping wet,
I would run up the winding hill that took
me to the bluff overlooking the Hudson
River and, in bare feet, follow a group into
the museum. I puzzled through the marble
and stone rooms, pondered the alabaster
statues of Jesus and Mary. I didn't dare
enter the chapel with a large crucifix — not
because of my bathing suit and bare feet,
but because at age seven or so I already
knew that I was an outsider.

There was a lot I didn't know; for example, where the lines were drawn between Jew and non-Jew. Did only Jewish
kids play the card game *pisha paysha,*
which depended solely on luck? Were all
pushcart vendors on the Lower East Side
Jewish? Was it sinful when my best friend,
half Hawaiian Chinese, half Caucasian,
lent me her rosary to keep me safe as I
walked up four flights from her ground-
floor apartment to mine?

Adding to my confusion was the occasional encounter with other children or
grown-ups. What *are* you? a kid across the
street asked me. Jewish, I said.

— You're going to go to hell, then.

— No I'm not.

— Yes you are.

— That's what *you* think.

It seemed unlikely that hell was so exclusive, the province of Jews alone.

And then, one Sunday morning, when I was roller-skating down our block, wearing what we used to call dungarees, a woman with a pink coat and a straw picture hat stopped me. Why aren't you in church on Easter? she demanded. I was dumbstruck. She prodded. I answered.

— I don't go to church.

— Of course you go to church. Is that where your parents are now? Easter is the most important day of the year.

— No. We don't go to church.

She probably narrowed her eyes.

— What *are* you? A heathen?

— I'm Jewish.

— No, you're not. You're lying. (She pointed to my face.) Those freckles, your hazel eyes, how could you be Jewish? What are you?

Up until then, I didn't know that Jews didn't have freckles or hazel eyes. You, what are you? I asked, trembling. She didn't respond as an uncle of mine might have: What are you, a wiseacre?

What was I? A kid who took being Jewish for granted. Passover was coming. I would help my mother take down the curtains to launder, the Passover dishes to wash. I was looking forward to matzo and macaroons. I was reading Nancy Drew mysteries that entertained me, though instinctively I knew she was not *one of us*. A few years later I would finally read books that spoke to my heart: *Marjorie Morningstar* and *A Stone for Danny Fisher.*

I was Jewish, all right, but I hadn't defined myself — a journey that would take several decades and that included belatedly learning enough Yiddish to keep up with the main character of a novel I would create. Definitely I grew up Jewish, but the truth is, I'm still growing.

> The Jew has made a marvelous fight in this world, in all the ages, and has done it with his hands tied behind his back.
> — Mark Twain

Lisa Solod

Lisa Solod's work has appeared in many magazines and newspapers. She was a fellow at the Virginia Center for the Creative Arts in 2000.

Growing up Jewish in the South isn't like growing up Jewish in much of the rest of the United States. Even nearly fifty years after my birth, when I tell people I come from east Tennessee, they are astonished. It doesn't help that I don't have a real Southern accent (my New England–born and –bred parents saw to that!), although vestiges of it do remain. "Surely Jews don't live in east Tennessee!" people always insist. But they did, and they do, still. Many of them, in fact, live in Knoxville. But that, unfortunately, wasn't where I grew up, although that city served as the Big City to which we went for nearly everything interesting and to which my family and a few others traveled, each and every Sunday, for religious education. I grew up in the much smaller, far more provincial town of Morristown.

Morristown served as the proving

ground for my life as a Jew and shaped everything about who I am as a Jewish woman. In fact, sometimes I wonder if I would feel as strongly an identity as I do were it not for the fact that, all through my youth, I was forced constantly to confront who and what I was. And yet, to many, the stories I tell of anti-Semitism and misunderstanding are as unbelievable as the very fact of where I come from. Not in America! Right?

The Jewish community in Morristown was very small and, thus, very tight. I understand that now there are only one or two (if that) Jews left there at all, the kids having grown and gone and the parents having retired elsewhere. We stuck together in spite of the fact that some of us didn't like each other very much and most of us had little in common other than our religion. We probably wouldn't have been friends had we been members of a large community in which to find people of like mind and spirit, but tossed together in the mixed salad of every possible denomination of Christians possible (from Holy Rollers to four or five different kinds of Baptists, to Presbyterians, Episcopalians, Methodists, Lutherans, Church of Christ, Pentecostals . . . you name it), we stood out. Our only compatriots were the Catholics, who were nearly as keenly misunderstood and of whom the other Christians were equally wary. Which explains why my parents' parties always included the Catholic priest, who had just finished a four-year vow of silence and must have been very glad indeed to have someone to talk to.

I have to say that in spite of my parents' ambivalence about living in the South in general, they handled the numerous incidents that befell my sisters and me with common sense and the proper amount of outrage mixed with self-deprecating humor. When, at six years of age, I came home from first grade crying about how I was going to go to hell because I didn't believe in Jesus, my mother took me in her arms and soothed me with the fact that if it were true that I was going to hell I (which she did not believe for one moment), once I got there, she, my father, my sisters, my grandparents, and so many others would all be there with me so that hell became a place of possible solace rather than a place to fear.

Over the years I was confronted with teachers who insisted on our raising our hands if we went to church on Sunday (temple did not count) and who then counted out gold stars to stick beside our names (of which I got none), and who forced us to recite the Lord's Prayer and sing "Jesus Loves Me" each morning before class. I took music classes far before the enlightened times of today when Hanukkah songs are de rigueur for holiday programs, and sang my heart out, being sure to stay silent during any mention of Jesus. My parents had confrontations with school principals who refused to excuse us for religious holidays and teachers who insisted we pray with the class each day during homeroom. Other children asked to see my horns and my cloven feet, and I was told each Passover that this was the holiday in which I killed baby boys and drank their blood. Right?

Periodically, especially during my high school years, tent revivals would come into town and huge numbers of young teenagers would be "saved" with great fanfare and excitement. They would then come back to school "heaven bent" on saving me. At least until the next Saturday night and the next beer-and-necking drive-in date.

But if I grew weary of the silliness and the slurs, I did not find myself a true outcast. I had friends, a good social life, a world in my books, and the absolute knowledge that I would eventually leave Morristown and find somewhere in which to feel comfortable (and I did). Somehow, even though I was different, I was different in so many ways, and with such a vengeance, that hate didn't come into the way people treated me. It was more often than not pure ignorance coupled with the sureness of being right that most kids' parents had drilled into them. Once in a while, I even got through to a kid or two, but mostly the incidents petered out as kids grew into teenagers and things like pimples, hair, makeup, cars, and all the important stuff took precedence over wondering which God was the best to serve.

It took me more than a few years to become this philosophical about my upbringing: The slurs and comments hurt. And, like most people, I hated being labeled "different" when I was sure I was as normal as anyone else. But I was, am, and always will be different. I know that now. And I know that being Jewish is only part of that.

I live once again in the South and am raising Jewish children here. Things are usually easier than when I was growing up, but every once in a while something happens to remind me of my past. When I gave a talk on Judaism at a local country church (at the request of my dental hygienist who innocently wondered what kind of sacrifices we Jews made in this day and age. "What?" I wanted to say. "You mean, like living in a town with no Bloomingdale's?"), I found many of the older women sitting very intently, listening to me talk about the historical foundations of Judaism (trying as I was to stay clear of anything too controversial). I thought I had made a large impact, and I had. Just not in the way that I thought. I was the first Jew the women had ever met in their lives.

For American Jews raised in large cities and urban areas, it's hard to imagine what it must be like to be the parent who drags the menorah to class each December, who explains to her children's friends just why it is we don't really celebrate Christmas, who shakes her young daughter awake each and every Sunday morning to put her in the car for that long drive down the road to religious school — just as I made the same trip forty years ago. But it's neither good nor bad; it's neither here nor there. It just *is*. Jews live all over the United States and, indeed, much of the world besides Israel. Living where I did as a child, living where I do now as an adult, makes me conscious every day of who I am and where I come from. Being a Jew in the South is an act of will; it's not easy and sometimes doing it right is a lot of work. But I never escape it. And for that, I am grateful.

> Everyone is kneaded out of the same dough but not baked in the same oven.
> — Yiddish Proverb

Sheriff of the Ship

Shecky Greene

Shecky Greene has performed at many Las Vegas hotels. He has also appeared on television shows such as *Roseanne* and *Mad About You*, as well as in films including Mel Brooks' *History of the World: Part I* and *Splash*.

Being Jewish is not a religion; it is a way of life — you learn how to eat bagels, lox, pastrami, and corned beef, and enjoy the smells of all that wonderful food that kills you before you turn forty-five.

I used to ask my mother, "Why do you make the chicken so greasy?" And she replied, "I don't make chicken. I just make a pot of grease and shape it like a chicken."

There is anti-Semitism everywhere. When I was in the service, there were guys from all over, from New York and from the South, and sometimes I got a little tenuous about being Jewish. One time aboard the ship, a Southern guy about six feet four inches tall asked me, "Before you get in the bunk next to me, what the hell are you?" I replied, trembling, "Whatever you want me to be." "Mormon," he said. So there I was, the only Mormon in the United States Navy who wore a six-pointed star. I told them all, "I am the sheriff of the ship."

In this life, I'm glad I was a Jew. When I come back in another life, I want to be a Jew. The only thing is now I have to break up my relationship with Mel Gibson.

There's no business like Jew business.

Gene Saks

Gene Saks is an actor and Broadway musical director who has appeared in such films as *Deconstructing Harry* with Woody Allen, and *I.Q.*, with Meg Ryan.

If you are a Rothschild, a Rosenwald, a Gimbel, or even a Waldbaum, growing up Jewish can be a rich experience. For the rest of us, it could be just so-so. Sholem Aleichem wrote *It's Hard to Be a Jew* (I imagine he had his payess pulled more than a few times), so it's natural that many of us play down our origin and do our best to integrate.

Some of us shorten our names or our noses or both. Others go further — they get tattooed and buy a pickup truck with a rottweiler in the back and hang out at the nearest 7-Eleven. I burnt my Hanukkah candles at both ends. I wore my kilts to my bar mitzvah. A fraternity brother became a Mennonite, moved to Pennsylvania, drove a horse and buggy, and lived in a barn with a hex sign.

We Jews can be extremely neurotic and are inclined to become easily depressed.

Most Jews seldom say, "Have a nice day," or even have one. To be honest, I've never heard a Jew say that. We're just not that optimistic. Life is neither a bed of roses nor a bowl of cherries. The best we can ever hope for is a dairy restaurant.

❦

A Jew in Texas

Fred Zeidman

Fred Zeidman, a Houston business-man, is chairman of the United States Holocaust Memorial Council, the governing board of the United States Holocaust Memorial Museum, in Washington, DC.

Wharton, Texas, population nine thousand, is not a Jewish metropolis. The resources of a Brooklyn or Baltimore — a kosher butcher, several shuls to suit people of different religious tastes, or a JCC at which to gather — were unavailable when I was growing up in the 1950s. It was not, to say the least, the type of place you'd expect to produce a future chairman of the United States Holocaust Memorial Museum.

But we had something special in Wharton,

something specifically relevant to the task of Holocaust remembrance, a quality those raised in the once-vibrant network of Jewish communities in the rural South cherish and one from which larger Jewish populations might learn a great deal.

We had each other. In fact, we didn't have much else.

In Wharton, there weren't quarrels between Orthodox and Conservative, or Conservative and Reform. There was no synagogue the next neighborhood over in which we'd never set foot. There was one for the whole town. I guess you'd call it Conservative, and the rabbi whose knees I learned at — a brilliant man who arrived in Wharton after surviving the fires of the Holocaust — tilted toward an Orthodox style. But that one shul, and that one rabbi, had to take care of everybody.

When the kosher meat was shipped in, packed in ice, from San Antonio, Houston, or even farther away, we drove together to pick it up. Folks carpooled thirty, forty miles or more to attend Hebrew school. If you wanted to be Jewish in Wharton, you had to work at it — a skill that we grew up to value when we moved to larger, more assimilated cities.

To say Wharton's Jewish population had

each other isn't to say we stood apart from the rest of the town. Quite the contrary: Folks of just about every ethnic stripe learned to get along because we had to.

There wasn't a Jewish neighborhood where we could seclude ourselves. Nor was Wharton a melting pot where everyone mixed together and lost the identities they came with. A small town is more like what folks across the Sabine River in Louisiana would call a gumbo: Everything in the kitchen sink gets tossed into the stewpot and has to figure out how to make it together.

There was anti-Semitism, to be sure. My parents warned me. "You're going to hear things about Jews," they explained. "Don't believe them. Be proud of who you are."

We didn't hear much, at least not explicitly. The synagogue was never damaged, either. Most of the anti-Semitism was subtle. Jews weren't allowed to join the country club until it went belly-up broke and they came looking for Jewish business owners to bail them out. My dad, who owned the town clothing store, replied that if he wasn't good enough for them when times were booming, they ought not come knocking during a bust. And it was my twenty-fifth or thirtieth high school reunion before it dawned on a friend and me that there were certain people's houses we were never invited to growing up.

But whenever I felt the antagonism, there was home — that magical threshold where a mezuzah on the doorpost was a gateway to a world steeped in Judaism inside. Only later in life — when those values, that determination to work at being Jewish, the ability to get along with just about anyone — would I appreciate the enormous sacrifices my ancestors and so many others made to build a Jewish life in the South.

What does that have to do with Holocaust remembrance? The notion of sacrificing to be a Jew — of working at it, of Judaism being a gift to be cultivated and embraced rather than taken for granted — that is among the greatest legacies and greatest miracles left to us by the Jews of Europe.

Their sacrifices are a compelling reminder of the high responsibility borne by those of us fortunate enough to live in safer times. If they could keep Judaism alive in the crucible of the Holocaust, surely we have a responsibility to do so today. That takes effort, to be sure. But the effort it took to be Jewish in Wharton is nothing compared to what was required in Warsaw.

They shut down the Wharton shul a couple of years ago. It's been folded into a larger congregation in Houston, and most of the remnants of Wharton's Jewish community have moved away. But the lessons will live in me forever — and they will inform my work with the United States Holocaust Memorial Museum for as long as I have the privilege to serve.

Riches from the Mameloshen

Larry Katzman

Larry Katzman's *Nellie Nifty, RN* cartoon is nationally syndicated and appears in newspapers and magazines in twenty-one countries.

What a loss it would be if contemporary English did not include the wonderful Yiddish words passed along by those of us who grew up Jewish!

The immigrant grandparents of most of my generation spoke English to us but Yiddish to each other. We absorbed a great many Yiddish words in their company, seemingly by osmosis. Most Yiddish words have no equivalent English word, and thus come in mighty handy in succinctly expressing ourselves. They have therefore survived into the twenty-first century, used by both Jews and gentiles, becoming part of the English language.

There's no phrase more expressive of trouble than *"oy veh."* "Mazel tov" somehow seems warmer than "congratulations."

How many English words would it take, for example, to express *"nu?"* "So what's happening?" "What's new with you?" "What's the result?" None are exactly *"nu."* A "maven" is definitely more knowledgeable than an "expert." In the same vein, "ganef" is more expressive than "thief." What would the garment trade do without *"schmatte"?*

"Goy" is all-encompassing, covering everyone in the world who is not Jewish. How about the much-used "whole megillah," which covers every detail of everything? Somehow no English word is expressive of a "schlemiel." A "dope" or even "sad sack" fails to compare. A "schlemiel" is solely a "schlemiel."

In our youth, we pictured a "shiksa" as a beautiful blonde non-Jew who was no better than she should be and undoubtedly great in bed. (As we grew up, of course, we found that Jewish girls played no second fiddle!)

And it would be a poorer linguistic world without *"toches"* or "tush"!

❦

On Not Having a Christmas Tree

Susan Davis

Congresswoman Susan Davis represents the Fifty-third District of California in the U.S. House of Representatives.

By the end of November my mother would brace herself for the onslaught of my pleas and whines about wanting a Christmas tree. It wasn't that I didn't feel good about being Jewish, but, in my city of Northern California where I knew only a handful of Jewish families and did not have a close friend who was Jewish, I did feel on the outs at the holiday season. All my friends had pretty, colorful trees, and their modest homes were decked out in red and green splendor.

One Christmas my mother finally relented. On Christmas Eve, she accompanied me to a tree lot after all the choice trees were gone. I spotted a lonely looking, small pink tree and purchased it with my savings. I was allowed to put it downstairs out of the view of my family. I decorated it and visited it every day. It was mine and it was the beginning of a realization that I didn't really need a tree to feel accepted and part of holiday cheer.

I tell this story because the experience helped me find my place and desire to celebrate even more what I had to bring of my Jewishness to my family and my friends. I found special meaning not only in celebrating Hanukkah at that time of year but also in telling the Passover stories and experiencing other Jewish celebrations. Later, it fostered my desire to attend the Brandeis Bardin Institute and be a counselor there. The lessons I learned contributed, also, to my journey to Israel to work on a kibbutz when the new state of Israel was nineteen years old. I was twenty-one.

***

Not Quite "Normal"

Len Berman

Len Berman is an award-winning, New York–based NBC-TV weekday sports anchor whose "Spanning the World" segment appears monthly on NBC's *Today* show.

It never seemed unusual to me to be Jewish. I grew up in Astoria, Queens, and most of my friends were Jewish. The same group of kids went through elementary and junior high school together in the same class. In addition, most of us went to Hebrew school together. And when it was time to go to high school, a bunch of us (mostly Jewish) went to Stuyvesant High School. We had a barbershop quartet, three-quarters Jewish, and the same three made the All City Chorus. Even at college (Syracuse University), most of the kids in my fraternity were Jewish. So the concept of being Jewish seemed normal.

Then I joined the army.

Actually, it was the New York National Guard, but part of the deal was to go to army basic training at Fort Benning, Georgia. It was not unusual to fall out into formation at four-thirty a.m. in the cold morning. I remember one morning when the platoon was standing in formation and the drill sergeant called out your name, and you had to respond by calling out your religion. One hundred and ninety-four guys yelled out "Southern Baptist." Six of us kind of coughed a muffled "Jewish" into our hands. Needless to say, it felt rather uncomfortable. Afterward I was approached by a fellow soldier, a big strapping black kid from Mississippi. He had never met a Jewish person before, and he asked me if all the other Jewish people were like me. Were there female, older, and younger Jews as well? I explained to him that Jews were normal people.

Somehow I didn't feel "normal" that morning.

<hr />

The Hebress of the Class

Ruth Knafo Setton

Ruth Knafo Setton is the author of the novel *The Road to Fez*. Her writing has appeared in many anthologies and journals and has received a number of literary awards. She is writer-in-residence for the Philip and Muriel Berman Center for Jewish Studies at Lehigh University.

"What does the Hebress of the class have to say about the New Jerusalem on the Hill?"

The Hebress of the class had nothing to

say about the New Jerusalem or about anything else in Mr. Minster's seventh-grade history class. Eyes lowered, I wished I was anywhere in the world but this dingy classroom, listening to gaunt, creepy Minster rave about the wisdom of Cotton Mather and mutter under his breath about the unspeakable practices of everyone in American history except the Puritans. "Sin" was his favorite word; everything we studied seemed to cover "a multitude of sins," particularly that mysterious group, the Hebrews — of which I was the sole representative. Endlessly fascinated by my mere existence — a real Jew — he circled me, scrutinized me, posed trick questions in an attempt to trap me into revealing the unspeakable practices of Jews. Worst of all, he never called me by my name: "What does the Hebress have to say about witch trials? Baking with blood? As we know, that covers a multitude of sins."

Everyone snickered, and at recess the kids yelled, "Hey, Hebress! Show us your unspeakable practices!"

An Ichabod Crane–like figure, always dressed in black with an uncommon number of buckles on his jackets, trousers, belts, and shoes — just like his heroes, the Puritans — Minster loomed over us, twining his long bony arms into pretzels. As he spoke, he had a repellent habit of swallowing with his tongue bunched up in his mouth so he looked like a frog devouring a lizard. His class was agony. The instant I heard his hollow voice intone the word "Hebress," I became tongue-tied. In my dreams at night he transformed himself into a demon who tracked me through deserts and across seas.

He trembled with excitement the day the blind girl came to visit our class. An older woman led her in and blocked the door, arms crossed over her chest, as if daring us to escape. The girl sat stiffly in a chair at the front of the room. She was about our age, eyes sealed shut, chin angled forward.

"Welcome, blind girl," said Minster. "Class, you will rise and shake hands with her."

Desks and chairs squeaked as we stood and lined up, whispering and giggling. No one stepped forward.

"She can't see you," snapped Minster. "Show the quality of mercy. Move closer. Shake her hand."

The blind girl was pale and pasty, with coarsely chopped black hair sticking up in points and tufts over her ears and collar. This detail made me inexpressibly sad.

How would it be to live your life without ever really knowing what you looked like? To have to rely on others to tell you there was food between your teeth or your hair was a mess?

"Blind since birth," said Minster, a tone of odd glee in his voice. "God has His ways, which are impenetrable to all but the initiates. And that covers a multitude of sins." He did a repulsive tongue roll, chin bulge, tongue flick.

I dragged my feet until I was last in line. I didn't want to show mercy and shake her plump hand. I'd never touched a blind person before, never even seen one. She was my first. I was scared. Of what? That she'd communicate her blindness to me? I shuffled my feet, stared at the grimy brown linoleum. Before me the line dwindled as students said their names, shook her hand, and hurried back to their seats. She tilted her head to one side, listening.

As I approached her chair, the air grew thicker, clotted with my fear. Her face was soft as the Pillsbury Doughboy's — the kind you poke with your finger, and it bounces back. Her black lashes were gummed together, a slit of light peeking through.

There were two more kids in line before

me. Suddenly I knew I couldn't touch her. If I did, something terrible would happen. I glanced up, and my breath caught in a gasp. Minster was staring directly at me with his evil squinty eyes, his tongue bunched and bulging.

My heart jolted in my chest. I retreated a step. I couldn't hear, couldn't think. Red dots hovered before my eyes. Suddenly the two kids before me were gone. It was my turn.

"Come on," said Minster. "We don't have all day. The blind girl has other classes to visit."

Why didn't I know her name? Who was she? She held out her hand, waiting. Her fingers were pudgy and pale, like her face. Her fingernails, bitten so low it hurt to look at them.

"Blind girl," said Minster, "meet the Hebress of the class."

I knew there was no escape. Bolting forward, I took her hand in mine. Her grip was surprisingly warm and firm. "Hello," she said.

"Hello," I said.

She let out a little snort, shook my hand harder. "Hebress." Another little snort. "Welcome to the tribe."

"You too?" I asked.

"Me too." Smiling faintly, she released my hand. Without thinking, I reached out and quickly smoothed the points and tufts of her hair. "It's sticking up," I said.

"Thanks. Bye." Her voice was wistful.

"Bye." Mine was, too.

I felt Minster's evil eye on me as I returned to my seat, but I didn't look up. The Hebress and the Blind Girl, I thought, and let out a little snort. The first seeds of rebellion had already begun to sprout. In the years to come they would blossom, bloom, tangle in jungle profusion, but that's another story, one filled with unspeakable practices, yea, one that covers the veriest multitude of sins.

> There are weapons that are simply thoughts. For the record, prejudice can kill and suspicion can destroy.
> — Rod Serling

Growing Up Jewish in Atlanta

Stuart Eizenstat

Stuart Eizenstat has served as under-secretary of state for economic, business, and agricultural affairs; under-secretary of commerce for international trade; the U.S. representative to the European Union; President Jimmy Carter's assistant for domestic affairs and policy, and executive director of the domestic policy staff at the White House. He currently practices law in Washington, DC.

Growing up Jewish was the major foundation for my life. But I did not simply "grow up Jewish," I grew up Jewish in the South. And this was a distinctive experience, being a religious minority at a time when a racial minority, Atlanta's black community, was the victim of overt discrimination.

Although I was born in Chicago during the war years, my father, Leo, was born and raised in Atlanta, Georgia, the capital of the South and the center of the largest Jewish community in the Deep South. I moved to Atlanta when I was eight months old and grew up there in the 1940s, '50s, and early '60s. In my formative years, there were about twenty-five thousand Jews in Atlanta, a population that has exploded today to more than seventy-five thousand. There were then four synagogues; today there are more than thirty.

My grandfather, Esar Eizenstat, came from what was then known as White Russia (now Belarus) to Atlanta in 1904. The area to which he moved, on the south side of the city — now around second base in Atlanta's baseball stadium — was heavily Jewish and Orthodox. The accent of the area was less Southern than Yiddish. He was very learned and observant, and passed those traits along to my father.

One story that has become a legend in our family involved my grandfather's Atlanta roots and Atlanta's premier institution, Coca-Cola. My father, then a young boy, remembers a well-dressed man coming to the door and engaging my grandfather, who spoke halting English, in an animated conversation. After my grandfather finished the discussion and closed the door, my father asked him who he'd been talking to. My grandfather said it was a salesman. When my father asked what the man was selling, my grandfather said it was stock in Coca-Cola. When my father asked innocently why he had not bought the stock, then being sold for pennies, my grandfather replied in his native Yiddish, *"Vayl keyner vet veln trinkn kolirteh vahse!"* (Because no one will drink colored water). My sons, Jay and Brian, have often laughed at how our family circumstance would be different if my grandfather had bought only one share of Coca-Cola early in the twentieth century.

Atlanta's Jewish community was still significantly divided along old European geographic lines. The German Jews largely lived in the northwest section of the city and belonged to the Temple, a Reform congregation that in my formative years did not permit the wearing of tallit or *kipot,* nor allow bar and bat mitzvahs. Reform Jews belonged to the Standard Club. Conservative Jews, largely of Eastern European origin, had their own congregations, Shearith Israel and Ahavath Achim (the AA, as it was called), the synagogue to which my family belonged. The AA was then, and is today, the largest Conservative congregation in the Deep South. Conservative Jews belonged to the Mayfair Club and Progressive Club. The separation between the communities was quite rigid. There was a small but significant Sephardic population with its own congregation.

I can remember only two anti-Semitic incidents growing up. One occurred when I was coming home from Hebrew school at the AA and was beaten up by the Taylor brothers, neighbors across the street, who also threw my Hebrew books away. The other was when my mother, Sylvia, drove me and a friend to Mooney's Lake for an outing. When we got there, we saw a large sign on the lawn near the lake that proclaimed, no jews or negroes allowed. The hanging of Leo Frank in 1913 was still a topic of discussion in the Atlanta Jewish community.

But the civil rights movement in the early 1960s shook the Jewish community. Before then, Jews in Atlanta and throughout the South, in my father's and mother's generation, generally took a low profile on civil rights for blacks. Jewish morals lost out to the laws of segregation. The Atlanta Jews kept their heads down, lest they become the object of bigoted anger. I learned how easy it is to accept a given order, even when it is unjust. I went to a segregated high school, never played basketball on the Grady High School team against any black high school team (I was an all-city and honorable mention all American basketball player at Grady, but I have always said that these honors should be with an asterisk, since I played in a segregated league!), and simply accepted this as a matter of course.

As a young boy, my parents took me to see the Brooklyn Dodgers play an exhibition game against the Atlanta Crackers, when the Dodgers were returning from spring training in Florida. Jackie Robinson was a star on the team. It was a big event for a black player even to be permitted to play in the Cracker stadium. Yet it caused me no moral pain that there was segregated seating, with blacks in small, uncomfortable bleacher seats way behind right field.

I remember the "Whites Only" drinking fountains and restrooms in places like Rich's and Davidson's department stores, yet simply took it for granted.

I also remember failing an early moral test. I was coming home on the Atlanta city bus one day from the AA synagogue, and an elderly black lady laden with bags boarded, looking for a seat. I was seated in the last row of the white section of the bus and there were no seats available for her in the small, cramped rear section allocated to blacks. I struggled with my Jewish conscience and with the mores of the time about whether to relinquish my seat to her. I simply could not break with convention and the "law" against integrated seating, and so I let her stand. As late as 1959,

Georgia Governor Ernest Vandiver threatened to close the public schools of the state rather than follow the edicts of the federal courts, following the Supreme Court's landmark decision against segregation in *Brown* v. *Board of Education.*

When Jews did get out front in the civil rights movement, like Rabbi Jacob Rothschild of the Temple in Atlanta, there was a price to pay. The infamous Temple bombing was a message that Jews should not support the civil rights movement. Yet, in fairness, Atlanta was the most tolerant of Southern cities in the 1950s and 1960s. It had progressive mayors, like William Hartsfield, Ivan Allan, and Sam Massell (Atlanta's first Jewish mayor and one of the first in a major city in the South). Atlanta's business community wanted at all costs to avoid the Bull Connor image of its sister community, Birmingham. Atlanta called itself "the city too busy to hate." There were major civil rights demonstrations against Atlanta institutions like Rich's Department Store, whose Magnolia Room refused to seat blacks. As late as 1962, when I was a sophomore at the University of North Carolina, I could not initially understand why black students from a nearby black college were sitting in, blocking access to a Howard Johnson's restaurant to which my fraternity brothers and I often went. When the realization hit me, it had a lifelong impact, making me a champion of civil rights for blacks and other minorities, starting from my college days through my support for affirmative action as President Jimmy Carter's chief domestic adviser in the famous *Bakke* Supreme Court case. But this was a belated recognition and since I was a member of a religious minority, one that should have come to me much earlier.

Most men of my father's generation were merchants who owned their own businesses or had individual professional practices that they could operate themselves. My father and his brother, my uncle Berry, owned their own wholesale shoe company, Berle Shoe Company. They were located on Pryor Street, and, later, in Fulton Industrial Boulevard, alongside almost exclusively Jewish merchants. My father's customers were small-business owners, all Jewish merchants in towns throughout the Deep South. He sold cheap shoes, *schmattes* as they were called in Yiddish. The bonds of religion and business between my father and his fellow Southern Jewish merchants were deep. He would come home with wonderful stories, which he would tell partly in Yiddish and partly in English. Once he told me about the sign he saw as he parked his shoe-filled station wagon in front of his longtime customer, "Benny's Shoe Store, located in a small Alabama town. The giant new sign read, BENNY'S, STORES ALL OVER THE COUNTRY!"

"How could you say this," my father inquired of Benny, "when your only store is in this one town?"

"Well," Benny explained, "there are stores all over the country. I didn't say they were mine."

Quotas were rampant in Southern colleges and universities well into the 1960s. One of my father's dearest friends, Joe Glazer, a brilliant Renaissance man, could not get into Atlanta's Emory Medical School and had to be satisfied attending Emory Dental School. There were few Jews in important law firms or banks. Indeed, even when I was applying to law firms in 1970, after graduating Phi Beta Kappa and cum laude from the University of North Carolina and then from Harvard Law School, with a tenure as a member of the White House staff under President Johnson (1967–68), and as the research director of Vice President's Humphrey's 1968 presidential campaign, as well as a federal judicial clerkship with Judge Newell Edenfield in Atlanta behind me, there were still major law firms that refused to consider me. I was selected by a major firm, Powell, Goldstein, Frazer & Murphy, where I spent more than twenty years (in Atlanta and later Washington), which had been founded by a Jewish partner in the early part of the twentieth century.

Judaism was a positive force growing up in Atlanta, not a source of negative concern. My whole environment growing up was suffused with Judaism. Although my father traveled all week selling his shoes around the South, he always came home in time for Shabbat dinner on Friday night, which my mother lovingly presented with candles, traditional food, and the blessings. After dinner, one of my earliest Jewish memories is of my father, himself very learned, taking out his Bible and sitting down with me on the couch in our den and going over the portion (*parsha*) of the week. He would read it in Hebrew and would translate aloud to me in English, to make the portion relevant and to help give it life and currency. I used that now-tattered Bible each of the four times I was sworn into office during the Clinton administration (ambassador to the European Union, undersecretary of commerce, undersecretary of state, deputy secretary of the treasury), to create a linkage with my father, to remember the lessons he taught me, and to remember my Jewish and Atlanta roots. My wife, Fran, and I also have adopted the practice for our own Shabbat dinners of discussing the weekly portion of the Bible and its relevance to our lives.

Ironically, one of the major gaps in my Southern Jewish background was the absence of any knowledge about the Holocaust. Even though both sets of my grandparents came from Eastern Europe, and my father and two uncles served in the U.S. military during World War Two, I never heard the Holocaust discussed when I was growing up, never to my knowledge met a Holocaust survivor, and never took a course on the Holocaust even in college — indeed, none were offered. It was only through experiences later in life that I became starkly aware of this enormous tragedy, which ultimately led me, decades later, to become special representative of the president and secretary of state on

Holocaust-era issues, negotiating massive payments for Holocaust survivors with Swiss, German, Austrian, and French companies and their governments.

But these gaps pale in significance to the importance that growing up Jewish in the South has had on me. It led me to a life of public service in order to give back to our great country what it had given to American Jews — the opportunity fully and freely to practice our religion and become part of the mainstream of American society. In my political career, I developed from my Southern Jewish upbringing a strong sense of the need to fight discrimination in all of its forms and a strong belief in the importance of affirmative action for African-Americans and other disadvantaged minorities. And my Jewish background created a feeling of the importance of *tikkun olam,* the need to do my part to "repair the world." But most important, Judaism has become a way of life for me, my wife, and my children and grandchildren, which has enriched our lives with the beauty and meaning of an ageless religious and cultural tradition.

> If only God would give me some clear
> sign! Like making a large deposit in my
> name at a Swiss bank.
> — Woody Allen

Fighting On

Barney Rosenzweig

Barney Rosenzweig is the Emmy
Award–winning executive producer of
Cagney & Lacey.

In September 1955, I was approaching my
eighteenth birthday and about to enter the
University of Southern California. I was in
for a shock. My hometown of Montebello,
California, was less than two dozen miles
from the urban Los Angeles campus of
USC, but for all the social and cultural differences I would encounter at my college of
choice, Montebello might as well have been
smack in the middle of rural Kansas.

Throughout my upbringing in that
working-class community of my childhood,
I remember only one single two-story
home, but at USC I had my first contact
with wealth, palatial estates, and the sons
and daughters of the rich and famous. My

129

schoolmates included the offspring of Walt Disney, Danny Thomas, Robert Young, Alan Ladd, Lew Wasserman, and Art Linkletter. It was also my first encounter with a bastion of political conservatism and a hotbed of flagrant anti-Semitism. This was something I would first learn of during rushing for the fraternity system at USC. As a "big man on campus" at my small hometown school, I was prepared — at least for a time — to be a little fish in a bigger pond; now I was learning that the "pond" was to be a segregated pool.

Only the Jewish fraternity houses were open to me. I met more Jews at one ZBT luncheon than I had ever seen in my entire life. My hometown, just on the outskirts of East Los Angeles, was a very secular and ethnically diverse community, and this kind of social regimentation made me uncomfortable. I decided against fraternity life, opting to remain an "independent." Initially I seemed to be doing fine. My first date on campus was with Barbara Young, the daughter of the man who had taught all of America that "Father Knows Best."

The date went well, I thought, but it was never repeated. Miss Young demurred at being escorted by me again. I later learned from her best friend from high school days that the Delta Gamma house, of which Miss Young was a pledge, fined their members $25 for dating Jewish men. (I never did get a quote on what it cost to date a black or Hispanic.) It was conceivable, of course, that Miss Young simply didn't enjoy our date as much as I did.

Miss Young's friend was JoAnne Lang, a lovely blonde girl of seventeen, who had been denied access to Kappa Kappa Gamma during rushing because, as the caller explained to her mother (who was married to two-time USC All-American footballer Aaron Rosenberg), "We're afraid that because of her stepfather, JoAnne will have Jewish sympathies that might infiltrate the house."

It wasn't only USC. In those days, in colleges all across America, there were quotas on the number of Jews admitted to the medical schools, to the dental schools, and to the law schools as well. Twenty years earlier, USC chancellor Rufus Bernard Von Kleinschmid had been an open and enthusiastic supporter of the German Bund movement. His disciples were peppered throughout the administration and the alumni organization for decades thereafter.

My mother had not gone out into the

workplace in order to earn the tuition for her oldest son to be exposed to such bigotry. She was beside herself. I had never seen her in such pain. She begged me to drop out and attend the state university across town, UCLA (Jew-CLA as some of my classmates at USC were fond of calling it in those days). She pleaded with me, "We'll take the money we save on tuition and buy you a Corvette!"

My mother was no slouch; this was a tempting bribe. The 1954–55 Corvette was a classic even then — a sure attractor of pretty girls. I was driving a 1941 Nash at the time and not having a lot of luck with the opposite sex. I sat on the edge of my bed, looking at my grieving mother. "I'm not quitting, Mom. I'm gonna stick it out, and someday I'm gonna own that school."

A little over three years later, in 1958, I was elected head yell leader of USC in an unprecedented electoral landslide. Considered to be the personification of the USC undergraduate, the "yell king" was the top student-body job on campus. I was the first Jew, and first nonfraternity man, in the school's history to hold the post and, in my senior year, Tommy Trojan, the famed statue in the center of campus, was renamed by the editors of the yearbook,

Tommy Trojanzweig.

My longest-term friends in life were made on that campus. Its favorable impact has lasted me throughout all my adult life, and I am more than comfortable with my contribution to change in the social fabric that is now ingrained in the tapestry of that school. This was reinforced for me nearly thirty years after my graduation when, at the ballroom of the Beverly Wilshire Hotel in Beverly Hills, because of the darkness in the room, I missed the look on my mother's face as I was given the University of Southern California's Alumni Award of Merit. To my delight, I am to this day mentioned (alphabetically, of course) in the official listing of USC distinguished alumni, just behind the actor John Ritter and ahead of General Norman Schwarz-kopf. Both the university and I have come a very long way.

In the Jewish Chapel

Sheilah Kaufman

A food writer and critic, Sheilah Kaufman has written twenty-four cook-books, including *Sephardic Israeli Cui-*

sine and *A Taste of Turkish Cuisine,* and serves as the online food editor for *Jewish Woman* magazine.

One "Jewish" experience that still makes me laugh took place at the Air Force Academy in Colorado Springs. A number of years ago, my husband and I and another couple decided to drive and tour Colorado, taking in all the beautiful and famous sites. When we got to the Springs, we wanted to see the Air Force Academy, and our primary goal was to see their chapels that represented the different religious denominations.

The academy offered tours, and we gathered with a group of approximately twenty non-Jews to see and hear about the different places of worship. Our tour guide was a very young, soft-spoken girl-woman who delighted in pointing out all the beautiful features of the various chapels. We could tell she took great pride in her job and in the beauty and distinguishing features of each chapel. When we finally ended up downstairs in front of the small but elegant Jewish chapel, she pointed out the magnificent Chagall windows, the Eternal Light, and a few other religious items. Since we had come to the end of the tour and were all standing around her in the hall, she concluded by pointing to the mezuzah. She carefully explained that it held a very special prayer for the Jewish people and finished by saying, "Notice it is slanted and points to the East — because Jesus will rise in the East!" And there we stood, four Jews with our jaws hanging practically to the ground.

They did not use me at all the first year after I won [the Miss America pageant]. The sponsors did not want me. And they asked me to change my name to Bess Merrick. I explained that I live in the Sholem Aleichem Apartment House with 250 Jewish families, and that no one would know who Bess Merrick is. We were like one family. When somebody was evicted, you took in a child, a mother, a bureau. So I should change my name? I am Louis and Bella Myerson's daughter.

— Bess Myerson

Martin Jay

Martin Jay is Sidney Hellman Ehrman Professor of History at the University of California, Berkeley.

On December 26, 1951, by order of the Supreme Court of the State of New York, Martin Evan Joslovitz was laid to rest. In his place, Martin Evan Jay was born. I was seven years old. The process of changing my name had long preceded my existence. My father, Joslovitz, an advertising executive from Far Rockway, had spent several years in the American hinterland, chasing after jobs during the Depression. In places like McKeesport, Pennsylvania, and Flint, Michigan, Joslovitz had proved something of a disadvantage. The shortened alternative stuck when he returned to New York, as attested by the marriage announcement when he wed Sarah Sidel in 1942 using the transitional name Jay Joslovitz.

Why the decision was made to lose the inherited name entirely almost a decade later I cannot explain, but I do recall feeling an enormous sense of relief. It was far easier, after all, for a seven-year-old to spell Jay than Joslovitz. But behind that simple reason, there lay a more fundamental explanation, which is self-evident to anyone familiar with the time-honored pattern of Jewish assimilation in America. Shedding an ethnically inflected name was still a means of upward cultural mobility in the middle of the twentieth century. Even seven-year-olds sense how these things work.

In retrospect, of course, what seemed at the time like a liberation feels a bit like a loss as well, but only a bit. For either through conscious choice or happenstance, the momentum of my integration into mainstream America has not lessened, and it would be disingenuous to deny that I feel comfortable with it. A crisis never accompanied the embrace of this new identity, nor did a compensatory reaffirmation of tribal roots follow at a later stage of my life. No nostalgia for "the world of our fathers" could, in fact, survive the resolutely unsentimental way the actual denizens of that world had talked about what they had so eagerly left behind.

But the Joslovitz within the Jay has never entirely disappeared. It has functioned as a shorthand reminder of the more profound linguistic traces that can still be discerned in my cultural subconscious. For growing up Jewish in midcentury New York meant being keenly aware of the palpable residues of the two languages that set us apart from our gentile counterparts. Yiddish, spoken fluently by grandparents and imperfectly by parents, served as a reminder of how recent the assimilation had been. Although rapidly receding from daily usage, it was still available as the secret tongue of those who did not want to be understood by their children or the punch lines of Borscht Belt comedians who provoked howls of laughter frustratingly denied those my age not in on the joke. Joslovitz came from that world with its apparent warmth, earthiness, and ethnic solidarity, however much these may be post facto projections. Its loss could easily be added to those others who have defined Jewish history written in the lachrymose mode since the fall of the Second Temple, a mode given immeasurable reinforcement by the horrible events in Europe fresh in everyone's mind.

The second "lost" language was, of course, Hebrew, in which I had been dysfunctionally trained by a bored former rabbi who came to my house every Wednesday afternoon for two years before my bar mitzvah. Although I learned to read the letters with a passable accent and catch some of the rhythms of the Haftorah passages I had to perform in front of the congregation, at no time was the language taught as a living tool of human communication. The opposite of Yiddish, it seemed the embodiment of a lifeless ritualism that had no connection to anything I might remotely find spiritually nourishing (or even nationally inspiring, as it was becoming in the newly created State of Israel). And yet, here too my inner Joslovitz could remind me of what it had meant for those who still proudly bore that name, like my observant grandfather David, whose regular synagogue attendance had not been emulated by his son or grandson.

Yiddish and Hebrew, like Joslovitz, had been allowed to pass into history, but they still disrupted my ability to feel fully at home in the linguistic world into which the seven-year-old Jay had been born again. There was always some dim sense that my native tongue had been native for only a scant generation before me. It has, of course, become a postmodernist cliché to celebrate the virtues of diasporic exile, intertexual juxtaposition, and linguistic heteroglossia (a kind of benign version of

Babel), but these were already somehow present in my cultural unconscious at a relatively early age.

Still, by the time I ventured out into the larger, mostly gentile world, going away to study at Union College, the London School of Economics, and Harvard, the transition from Joslovitz to Jay seemed pretty firmly established. But there one episode during my graduate student years that demonstrated its fragility. For reasons too complicated to rehearse now, I found myself at the other end of a phone call from the wife of the Washington columnist Joseph Alsop, as patrician a WASP as one might imagine. When she found out my last name, she was delighted. It was, she explained, her own maiden name. "Old Huguenot name," she proudly informed me, "and yours?" "Old Litvak name," I absurdly blurted in response.

Another anecdote gives the story a final twist. When I married in 1974, my wife decided not to adopt my last name. The reasons were varied: Feminism had made it a badge of honor to resist the automatic change of name, she had already begun establishing a professional identity, and her daughter by a previous marriage would still have the old name. But there was also another reason: Jay, she said, sounded too bland, too neutral, too lacking in ethnic resonance. In fact, it seemed too English in origin, and she would prefer not to be identified as English. And so she kept her own name — I will leave you to sort out the multiple ironies — Mary Catherine Gallagher.

Opening a New Door

Benjamin Cardin

Congressman Benjamin Cardin represents Maryland's Third District in the U.S. House of Representatives.

I grew up in the Ashburton neighborhood of Baltimore, which in the 1950s was almost entirely Jewish. As a youngster, I attended the neighborhood public school, which was open on Jewish holidays, but the classrooms were empty as students attended High Holiday services. I also remember that because my school was almost entirely Jewish, it was the Jewish students who participated in the annual Christmas pageant.

While we may have put on the annual Christmas show, it never occurred to me that everyone wasn't Jewish. That changed when I was around eight years old and I went door-to-door in my neighborhood collecting for the Jewish National Fund. I knocked on someone's door and was told that they weren't Jewish. I was shocked. I thought *everyone* was Jewish!

Chosen

Richard Marcus

Richard Marcus, best known for his role as Mr. William Raines in the television series *The Pretender*, is also a writer and producer whose works include *Parasite*, starring Demi Moore. He has acted on the television shows *St. Elsewhere*, *Highway to Heaven*, *L.A. Law*, and *Melrose Place*.

Gagliano.
Stamingo.
O'Mera.
Their names sounded like the mob muscle spawned in Hell's Kitchen and Five Points. But they were tougher than those thugs. And they wore makeup. They were my elementary school teachers. It was 1959.

Gagliano, Stamingo, and the red-faced O'Mera. Ah, O'Mera. Her rimless glasses and squat, angry, potato-shaped body hovered over me every day in anticipation of my next screwup. She was never disappointed.

By third grade, Miss Stamingo would send me to Principal Whitman's office without even the benefit of a trial. I understood why. I had already been tried and found guilty of everything for eternity in Miss Gagliano's lower court of second grade. Since my criminal record preceded me, there was no need to cover old ground. I was resigned to the fact that if there was any disturbance occurring within fifteen yards of my Sears and Roebuck–encased body, I was gone.

I spent so much time sitting in Principal Whitman's office that I like to think there's a velvet rope across that hard wooden chair on which my butt squirmed almost daily. Maybe even a small plaque with my name on it honoring my many years of service.

The *second* most heinous crime I ever committed was when I told Miss Stamingo — truthfully — that my rabbi ordered us to refuse to sing Christmas carols. I felt secure in the knowledge that, as Rabbi Gartner had assured us, our teachers would understand. Miss Stamingo did not understand. Her face became a frigid, white sheet of stone. In the corners of her mouth, bristling little powdered mustache hairs sprang to life. Her usually almost bored, singsong tone became hard, clipped. "That's too bad," she said. "You have such a nice singing voice."

As I trudged to Mr. Whitman's office (the only place she could think to send me), I figured not singing carols because I was Jewish must be a whole different way of being wrong.

I felt that my religious boycott was a courageous act on my part. Not because I was a nine-year-old who was inflaming the wrath of a woman whose rigorous indoctrination (and obligatory anti-Semitism) began in the less enlightened 1880s. It was an act of kid bravery because I *liked* Christmas carols. I liked to sing. And I *did* have a nice voice. In fact, except for the Jesus part, I liked Christmas. I mean, what did Jewish kids have? Hanukkah? Forget it. These days it's been super-sized. But back then Hanukkah was a minor, vaguely understood celebration. It fell into that category of Jewish holidays that could be summed up in one sentence: "They tried to kill us, we won, let's eat."

Hanukkah didn't have even one remotely catchy or inspirational tune. Even the most boring holiday song ever created, "I Had a Little Dreidel," had not yet been droned onto vinyl. Nobody dreamed of a white Hanukkah. Every Jewish kid knew that you could get a lot more presents under that tree than you could ever shove under a menorah. And with the Jewish parent/child negotiations stalled at the "eight nights = eight presents" rule, we were the "chosen people" except when it came to how much kids could choose from the F.A.O. Schwarz Christmas catalog. Which also didn't make sense that a guy named Schwarz would put out a Christmas catalog.

So you could say I was getting mixed messages about a lot of things. When they broke out the lyric sheets for "Silent Night" in O'Mera's class the next year I went to Whitman's office without even being asked.

Now, we all knew that for Stamingo and Gagliano, meting out punishment was merely part of the job description. They executed their obligations with detached, hit-man efficiency. But O'Mera seemed to castigate with a certain zeal. It was like she enjoyed it. It is one thing to be one of the "usual suspects." It's another when a teacher is gunning for you personally. Every morning I walked into her class, I fought the feeling that O'Mera wanted me to disappear. I realize, now, that it took grit for a little kid to enter a room, every day, knowing he was in the crosshairs of a one-woman firing squad. But back then I simply assumed I was wrong about everything, so this was just the way it had to be.

I'm not sure what minor infraction I was busted for that day. But I knew the drill: Up to her desk, head down, get chewed out, then listen to the slap and echo of my own footsteps down the empty, well-waxed hallway to the chair. But this time it felt different. She started to review the particulars of my *past* felonies. Then her voice got this weird sound in it. I heard her say that I was a troublemaker and always would be a troublemaker. Okay. We know this. I'd already been convicted of everything for eternity. Why bring it up? Just stamp my file with its current violation so I could hand it over to Warden Whitman.

Instead she turned to the class and announced that I was "insane" and went to "a doctor for crazy people." Then she looked at me as if she was waiting for me to, I don't know, explode? Melt? Admit I was a nutcase? I was fascinated. Not only because I felt the announcement of such a thing was a new level of cruelty and shame — she was always raising the bar on that score — but because she was *wrong*.

Those monsters in flower-print dresses were a lot of things — mean, hard, unforgiving — but to a kid in the 1950s they were never, *ever* wrong. Except that day, that one time. Hey, I'd certainly know if I was going to a doctor for crazy people. I didn't go to any doctor except for Dr. Hirsch. And every kid in town went to Dr. Hirsch. Miss O'Mera was *wrong*. And this thing she was saying was . . . the word popped into my head: *personal*. It didn't make sense. I was a kid. And kids didn't have anything personal about them. She obviously thought otherwise. And then it became obvious that she was trying to shame me in front of the whole class. She was trying to ruin my whole life with a lie. She was about to make every future recess and lunch and kickball game — previously off-limits to teachers' opinions and criminal records — a living hell.

Now, in the general prison population a troublemaker's rep bought you a bit of positive notoriety. But *really* wacko? Whoa. I'd known of a few. None of them branded officially, like this by a teacher, but rumor alone could demolish you. You were shunned. Invisible. Permanent cooties. I realized I was fighting for my life up there. And she was *wrong*. All I could do was something no kid had ever done. What did I have to lose? I was dead either way. I yelled back.

"I don't see any doctor! You are wrong!" It was a toss-up as to who was more surprised.

Miss O'Mera's usually florid countenance dropped several shades into a thunderhead of raging purple. I immediately flashed on Miss Stamingo's quiet, frigid mustache hairs. I would have welcomed them. O'Mera squawked that my being crazy was in a place called my "records" (it was on an album?!). Then she said I was seeing someone called a "psychologist." Now I *knew* she was lying. There was no grown-up I knew that had any name like "psychologist." Dr. Hirsch was a pediatrician. My dad's company had a superintendent named George, and my mom's friend Sandy was a dance therapist, but those were the most complicated grown-up names in my life. I felt an even stronger sense of purpose.

"You're wrong! I don't see anybody called a psychologist!" I yelled with all the fervor and truth I could marshal up into my stout little body. (I was also quite impressed that I pronounced "psychologist" correctly.) Sure, I was crying. I was terrified. I was taking on The Man. The System. Nurse Ratched. Then I had a sense of another force at work: The Class. They were hanging on every word. They weren't actually rooting for me (mobs hedge their bets till they see who's winning). I couldn't blame them. They were as scared as I was.

Miss O'Mera became more livid and insistent that I was a horrible, evil, psychotic troll (not her words exactly). I kept shouting my passionate denials. "Wrong! You are wrong!"

I could see the fascination on my classmates' faces. Nobody knew how this was going to turn out. A kid, an actual kid, was standing up to the injustice that was heaped upon all of us daily. I caught O'Mera's look. There was a flicker in her eyes and a pinched-lipped grimace of frustration. I stood my ground. Mostly because I knew I was right, but also because there was nowhere for me to go. She studied me hard for several moments. I would not have been surprised if she'd rolled up a newspaper and tried to whack me like a gnat. She straightened up. She let out the tiniest *pfft* of air. I knew what was coming next. I wondered if Whitman would even bother to come out and talk to me or would I just sit in the chair till I was sixty-five years old.

"Go back to your seat," she said. I was stunned. For a moment I didn't understand English. My seat? In the class? Then, I didn't know why I knew it, but I knew. I'd won. She had nothing on me. A *teacher* had made a mistake of gigantic proportions. And I'd stood my ground for truth and justice and the American way! Even if I was Jewish. Some other poor sucker was seeing whoever she said I was seeing. The class was dead silent as I went back to my seat. But I could tell they were in awe. Miss O'Mera went back to whatever it was the class had been doing: her slides of the Grand Canyon, or some trip she'd taken last summer with Miss Stamingo and Miss Gagliano. They were always taking trips together. I'd won. It felt great. It still feels great forty-three years later. Even after I realized, about thirty years ago, that the really nice guy, Mr. Mecklin, whom I went and talked to every Tuesday was probably a psychologist.

> No matter how bad things get, you got
> to go on living, even if it kills you.
> — Sholem Aleichem

The Permits

Steve Israel

Steve Israel represents New York's
Second Congressional District in the
U.S. House of Representatives and was
appointed assistant whip by the Democratic Caucus.

Two historic documents hang in my office
on Capitol Hill: the permits that my immigrant grandparents received after they arrived in Brooklyn from Russia near the dawn
of the last century.

I display those documents not for the
constituents and lobbyists and tourists
who visit my Washington office. Rather, I
have placed them on the wall immediately
next to my desk to help guide me through
difficult votes on controversial legislation.
The documents are a reminder of the
values and aspirations that brought my
grandparents across an ocean in search of
freedom and of the values that they helped

instill in me throughout most of my life. They remind me of where I came from and help me determine where our country is going.

The pictures on both official documents are revealing. Strangers in a new land with dark eyes that saw oppression and pogroms in Russia — but in these photographs remained wide to the possibility of a different and hopeful life in America.

The permits, now faded and brittle, initiated the American dream for my grandparents. They enabled them to find work and work hard. They built a family in Brooklyn. They raised two kids who raised five who are raising another five. They put some money aside and soon helped my own parents get through their own financial struggles — often by clandestinely depositing cash into my mother's pocketbook when no one was looking. Growing up with my grandparents, we were taught that money doesn't grow on trees but were led to believe that it magically grew in my mother's purse.

And as they grew into America, America grew into them. Grandpa Myron became a full-fledged political expert — a European-accented pundit who could shout down anyone appearing on Fox News those days with an opinion about everything: on Nixon, Vietnam, Watergate, the Republicans, the Constitution. Meanwhile, Grandma Rae would putter silently in the kitchen, cleaning and straightening, and softly pointing her grandchildren to the "candy drawer" stuffed with treats. In a sense, dinner conversation with my grandparents was a living memorial to the Bill of Rights: In America, we have the right to agree, the right to disagree, even the right to remain silent (which Grandma Rae clearly preferred).

Today those rights face threats in many different faces: not threats from the kind of violence and terror that my grandparents fled, but rather real and tangible threats to the kind of freedom and liberty to which they fled. Today in Congress we debate new laws that would restrict too many of our rights, not expand them. Today it is fashionable among many to vilify immigrants, even though virtually all of us can hang the same documents that I have placed on my walls. When Congress must decide on the proper responses to those challenges, I look at the two faces staring at me from those immigration permits and think about my grandparents, and the America that helped build their family, and how they built America. Growing up Jewish has enabled me to help determine our nation's future by drawing on the extraordinary values and work ethics of the past.

In his strong accent, Grandpa Myron used to repeat, "My country right or wrong, it is my country." When he took that picture after arriving here, could he ever have dreamed that America would not only become his country, but that one day his future grandson would serve in his country's Congress?

Only in America.

⁕⁕⁕

West Hartford

Jacob Neusner

Distinguished Research Professor of Religion and Theology at Bard College, Jacob Neusner has published dozens of books, the most recent of which is *Judaism: An Introduction*.

We moved to West Hartford, Connecticut, in 1937, when I was five, and the town had around nine thousand people, not many Jews. We lived at 1651 Asylum Avenue, between North Quaker Lane and Foxcroft Road, from then on. That is where I grew up, through Beach Park School, kindergarten onward through grade six; Alfred Plant Junior High School, grades seven through nine; and William Hall High School, grades ten through twelve. It was a happy life. But when I graduated from Hall High, I went off to Harvard and never came back to West Hartford again, except for a while for brief visits to see family, and never wanted to. I don't think I have been in West Hartford in maybe twenty, thirty years now, and I can't imagine going back.

If truth be told, I'm not sure why. Certainly anti-Semitism was a reality to be avoided or dismissed, but it was present. There were occasional minor anti-Semitic incidents, more frequent hostile remarks about Jews. America was a Jew-hating, Jew-baiting country at that time, and West Hartford restricted Jewish residence to only certain neighborhoods (after World War II, it was mostly north of Albany Avenue, so Bice Clemow of the *West Hartford News* told me at the time). We Jews more or less understood, moreover, that Jews did not look for jobs in insurance companies, except in sales, heavy industry (Pratt & Whitney, Colt, Pitney Bowes), the utilities, and so on. When I went to Harvard, an even 10 percent of my class was Jewish; Yale took many fewer, Princeton still fewer. But West Hartford was no worse than any other suburb anywhere, so I imagined. And Harvard was the deep freeze, anyhow; one got used to exclusion. Harvard did not make Jews feel welcome. It was a very personal thing: I never even met the master of Kirkland House, where I lived, an aristocratic classicist named Mason Hammond, who, in the tradition of his field in those times, liked Jews only a trace more than he liked poisonous reptiles.

Nor did we Jews lack weapons of self-defense and self-esteem — of a sort. My father was a proud Jew and used the *Connecticut Jewish Ledger*, which he had founded in 1929 and published until 1954 (after then my mother published the paper until she sold it to the staff in 1965), to defend the beleaguered community. I remember that in 1942 an anti-Semitic businessman in Hartford wrote a letter to the mayor, saying, "Praise the Lord and pass the Jews to Hitler and we'll all stay free." The *Ledger* printed that letter on the front page, and the Jewish community collected apologies for months afterward. My father didn't fear anybody, and neither have I — not then, not ever. I learned that the real costs lie in cowardice, not in courage, which is free.

No, it was not anti-Semitism that persuaded me to leave and never come back. It was something else. I didn't know it then, but I grew up odd man out. I was left-handed, a poor athlete (only in middle age did I turn myself into a swimmer, doing a half mile a day, every day, and now, at an ancient seventy-two, into a jogger and weight lifter, of all things), and, alas, smarter than anyone I knew but not really aware of it. All I knew was that I was bored except when I was by myself, and then I was never bored. To this day, I daydream more than any other activity. That's why I'm never lonely and never bored.

Becoming an OD

Jerome Slater

Jerome Slater is professor emeritus at the State University of New York at Buffalo and a frequent contributor to the Jewish magazine *Tikkun*.

In 1957, fresh out of college and a year of graduate work at Yale, I joined the navy for three years as a junior officer assigned to a destroyer. In my first two years I was miserable. I was a rather bookish — nerdy? — and sheltered New York Jewish "intellectual," with little experience in the outside (i.e., goyish) world. Naturally I didn't fit in with my fellow officers, most of whom were either Naval Academy graduates or happy-go-lucky fraternity boy types. We didn't much like one another.

For a few months, until he finished his tour of duty, there was one other Jewish officer (and, so far as I knew, no enlisted men) on board my ship, LTJG Wally Fuller. Unlike me, Fuller had no problems: As a fun-loving, hard-drinking fraternity boy, he fit right in. Indeed, not only was he one of the boys among the officers, but the enlisted men in his division fondly painted a Jewish star on one of the ship's torpedoes.

In those cold but nonwar days, the main ambition of all junior officers was to qualify as officer of the deck. At sea, the OD served as the chief bridge officer and direct deputy to the commanding officer, whenever the CO was not on the bridge. To qualify, you went through an onboard junior OD training program in maneuvering, seamanship, and general operation of the ship. After nearly two years on board, I was the only eligible junior officer who had not even been assigned to the junior OD program. So I would obviously never become a bridge officer, one more mortification and indication of my low status on board.

One summer morning the ship was training a few miles off the coast of Miami Beach, then overwhelmingly Jewish. At dinner in the officers' wardroom that evening, the ship's captain, an unpleasant, alcoholic boor — let's call him George Leighton — sneered that from the bridge you could easily see "the chosen people." That was that for me — that evening I handed the ship's personnel officer an official request for a transfer.

Naval regulations gave anyone the right to request a transfer, which then had to be forwarded through the chain of command to the Bureau of Naval Personnel. Several weeks later I was ordered to report to the overall commanding officer of our squadron, consisting of eight destroyers. The squadron commander was Captain James P. Craft, a taciturn spit-and-polish Southern gentleman in the classic naval mode.

I reported to Captain Craft's office and stood at rigid attention before him as he sat at his desk. He had my transfer request in front of him and said that he was considering whether to recommend approval or not. He then asked why I had put in the request. I responded, vaguely, that I didn't think I had done very well, that in particular I had never even been assigned to the JOD program, and that I wanted a chance to do better in my last year in the navy. He stared at me, pondered a moment, and then asked, "Do you think that, ah, religion has anything to do with the situation?"

Evidently Craft had somehow learned about Leighton's remark. I had a split-second decision to make. I thought of Wally Fuller's success, and in any case I had no way of knowing whether Leighton knew that I was Jewish. So the truth was, probably, that it was not so much that I was Jewish but that I was different. Anyway, I think I also sensed that there was a right and wrong answer to Craft's question. I made my decision: "No, sir," I said.

Craft looked at me thoughtfully, nodded his head, and said this: "Ensign Slater, I'd like you to do me a favor. I want you to put this request on hold for a month. If you still want a transfer at the end of that time, I will forward your papers with a recommendation for approval. Will you do me that favor?"

"Yes, sir," I said. The next day I was assigned to the JOD training program — Craft, of course, was Leighton's immediate superior — and a few months later (by pure chance) Leighton finished his tour of duty and was replaced by a new commanding officer. I withdrew my transfer request. As it turned out, I learned quickly how to maneuver the ship and run the bridge, and I was also good at my main job as the ship's antisubmarine officer; not only that, the new CO liked me.

Consequently, I was soon designated an officer of the deck and was promoted in rank to LTJG as well. My status on board the ship improved dramatically, and in my last year in the navy I had a very good time. When I left, the officers threw a going-away party for me, at which the CO made a nice little speech, and I got very drunk. And a few years ago, along with untold millions of others who served in the military from 1945 to 1990, I received a citation from the Defense Department for having helped, personally, to win the cold war.

In the nearly fifty years that have passed

since then, I have come to believe that the moment I stood before Captain Craft was the turning point in my life. I think if I had seized upon the invitation to attribute my problems to anti-Semitism — whether correctly or not, who knows? — I would have been transferred to some dead-end shore job and finished my military service as a failure. And that would have weighed heavily on me, I am sure, for the rest of my life.

I never saw Captain Craft again — in the navy, that is. After finishing my naval service, I went to Princeton and got my Ph.D. in political science. In my last year in graduate school, I gave a paper at the annual meeting of the American Political Science Association, proudly wearing my "Princeton University" badge. As the meeting ended, I was still sitting at the front table when an older gentleman came up, patiently stood in front of me until I looked up, and then deferentially asked if he might have a copy of my paper. He looked vaguely familiar, so I looked at his badge: "James P. Craft, Lake Forest Junior College."

We had come full circle. I was too overwhelmed to say anything, and of course he didn't recognize me. Why should he?

Joel Siegel

Joel Siegel is film critic and entertainment editor for ABC-TV's *Good Morning America*. In his youth, he also served as a joke writer for Robert F. Kennedy and collaborated with Terry Gilliam of Monty Python fame.

I grew up with the Holocaust. I was born in 1943. My parents didn't try to hide the Holocaust from their little boy. They were young, in their early twenties, with family in Poland and Romania. No one then could have imagined what had happened to their families.

I grew up in East Los Angeles, Boyle Heights — think of the Lower East Side with stucco — where people came from everywhere and where I knew when I got old I'd speak with an accent; every old person did. I just didn't know what kind of accent: Jewish, Southern, Mexican, Irish, Italian, Chinese, Japanese. One day, it must have been 1948, I was in the first grade, and my reading group was talking about where we were born. I was born in Los Angeles; someone was born in Chicago; Lucille, on whom I had a crush, was born in New York. A Japanese girl, I think her name was Jeannie, said she was born in a concentration camp. I cried all the way home. I knew about concentration camps in 1948; I had family who died in them.

Fifty years later, I was watching *The Joy Luck Club*, a very good movie, and, during one scene, I started to sob so hard I almost doubled over. They were Chinese immigrants, living in San Francisco. A letter had come from their old country with news of the death of one of the girl's family. Raised American, she didn't speak Chinese, and the aunt who read the letter lied to her, told her everyone was fine.

I remembered almost the same scene taking place in my parents' bedroom just after the war. I guess I was three or four. All the women in the family were there, even Mrs. Fink, a very old, fragile woman, my mother's great-aunt; her high-pitched voice and soft Yiddish accent made her one of my favorites. They were reading a letter in Yiddish and crying.

"What's wrong, Mommy?" I asked.

"Nothing," she told me. "This is a letter from Poland that tells us everybody is okay."

The film brought it all back. My mother

was lying. This was the letter that told her that everyone had died: her grandparents, aunts, uncles, cousins. But, we'd learn a few months later, some survived. She got a letter from an American soldier stationed in Germany who had found one of her aunts, Dvaireh, and her two children, Sara and Itzhak, in a displaced-persons camp in the American Zone.

When Hitler and Stalin divided Poland in 1939, Pinsk, where my mother was born, ended up as part of Russia. Stalin arrested and sent to Siberia everyone in the Russian half of Poland who had any organizational skills: labor leaders, schoolteachers, priests, and my great-uncle Zyskind, Dvaireh's husband, who had been the secretary-general of the Zionist Party in Pinsk, a hotbed of Zionism where Golda Meir and Chaim Weizmann were born.

When you were sent to Siberia, your family went with you. Joe Stalin saved their lives.

After the war, Dvaireh and her children made their way to Israel, leaving Zyskind in the gulag.

Years later, Dvaireh wrote a letter to Mrs. Khrushchev: "You have my husband. He's served his sentence; you don't need him, but I do. He hasn't seen his children in twenty years; he has grandchildren he's never seen."

It worked. Mrs. Khrushchev intervened and I met Zyskind in Israel.

My uncle Muttie rounded up a couple of cartons of Luckies, which were as good as gold in postwar Germany, and sent them to the GI who'd sent the letter.

I remembered this, and when I remembered it to my mother, she started to cry all over again. "And you know," she said, "the soldier who sent the letter wasn't even Jewish."

In 1964 I went to Israel for the first time and met my family. I was a college kid, traveling through Europe with a college best friend, Steve White, on $100 a month. On a whim we decided to go to Israel. I wrote my mother to alert the family. We took a boat from Patras, Greece, to Haifa. The food was inedible, the hold was so dark that when they turned off lights it was like the gag the rangers pull at Carlsbad Caverns — you could not see your hand even when it was pressing against your nose less than an inch from your eyes. And there, as we marched off the gangplank, was my *tante* Dvaireh, my mother's aunt, armed with my high school graduation picture, checking the picture against the face of every passenger until she found me.

"Yossel?" she asked. "Yossele?"

We took the Haifa–Afula bus to the family's kibbutz, Kibbutz Yifat, where we'd milk cows and prune apple trees. One day I collected garbage and rued that there were no pigs to feed it to.

In America, we're newcomers, first generation, but our family in Israel is the equivalent of pilgrims. Two years after my mother and her parents and her aunt Rutke and their children came to America, her aunts who didn't have children, who were still teenagers, immigrated to Israel in the second aliyah.

Dvaireh was too young to come to Israel in the 1920s. She tried to come to Israel on the *Exodus*. The real *Exodus*, with her son, Itzhak, and her daughter, Sara.

The real *Exodus* was an overcrowded, rusting hulk of a ship that never made it past the British blockade. No one ever thought it would. A few days out of Italy one of the decks on the ship collapsed and a young man, *noch* a survivor, landed in Sara's bunk. That's how my cousin Sara met Dov Freiberg.

"I had to marry her." He laughed when he told me the story. He's been laughing at the story for fifty-five years.

"Maybe you wonder why we didn't fight back?" Dov asked me.

They lived in Ramla, a town near Ben-Gurion airport, and they still do, in a tiny, two-bedroom apartment they and their two daughters gladly shared with me and Steve. We were sitting on my bed — which doubled as the couch when my bedroom became the living room, which it did during daylight hours except during meal-times, when it was also the dining room — when Dov, nodding at the blue numbers tattooed on his forearm, asked the question and then surprised me by answering it.

"We did fight back," he said, with more sorrow than pride in his voice. "We did."

I can understand Yiddish but I don't really speak it. My Hebrew consists of calls to prayer and a few other words I picked up when I studied for my bar mitzvah: boy (*yeled*), girl (*yaldah*), and shut up (*sheket*). Dov's English was even worse than my Yiddish. But somehow we found enough words in common for him to tell me the story of Sobibor, the Nazi extermination camp where the Jews fought back, and Dov was one of them, where three hundred thousand Jews were killed and three hundred survived and Dov was one of them.

"I was fourteen when the war broke out," Dov began. He was a poor kid from Lodz, Poland. I never asked about his family, whether he'd had brothers or sisters. When the Jews were forced into the ghetto, Dov escaped, then escaped back into Lodz because there was no place to go. When they were sent to Warsaw, he escaped again, then escaped back into the Warsaw ghetto because there was no place to go. Then he was sent to Sobibor, one of three Nazi extermination camps. Because he was young and healthy, he wasn't killed outright but was chosen to be part of the cadre. He stacked suitcases carried by Jews who thought they were going to work camps; he clipped hair and pulled gold teeth from their corpses.

"You know what the most valuable thing in the camps was?" he asked.

"Diamonds?" I guessed. "Gold?"

He shook his head. "A *leffel,*" he said in Yiddish. A spoon.

If you had a spoon, when they let you eat you could eat like a human being.

In Sobibor, in all the camps, there was a place the Jews called "Canada" — a land of riches where clothing, jewelry, even food taken from victims was warehoused. One of the guards there, Dov remembered, wanted to see if Jews could fly. "He'd have us climb on the roof, then jump off using an umbrella as a parachute. I was a skinny kid. I fell; I didn't get hurt."

He told me about another guard, an officer, Stengel was his name. He would chase Dov through the camp, using a whip and shouting, "Run, run, child of Israel. Maybe you'll run to Palestine." A year after he told me his story, I read they'd caught Stengel, working at a Volkswagen plant in Brazil. Dov testified at his trial. Stengel recognized him. "I should have killed you," he said to Dov from the witness stand, "when I had the chance."

Dov testified at the Eichmann trial. After he testified at a war crimes trial in Frankfurt, a group of young Germans followed him back to his hotel and beat him. "I told them," he told me, "I survived worse."

"I had typhus," he told me. "I had a fever, I couldn't work, I hid. The guard who found me beat me, whipped me. I don't know how, but his beating cured me. I felt better."

The Dutch-Jewish community was exterminated at Sobibor, as well as Russian-Jewish prisoners of war. When the Nazis captured American or British soldiers, the Jews were almost always treated as POWs, which at least gave them a chance. When the Nazis tried to segregate "Jewish personnel" — "all Jews step forward" — there are hundreds of stories of whole companies of men risking their own lives, all stepping forward. But the Nazis treated Russian-Jewish prisoners as Jews.

At Sobibor that would be the Nazis' downfall.

"One day a Russian paratrooper came into the camp. A major" — he pronounced it with a hard "g." "An officer, six foot tall, head shaved bald. He looked around, saw what this was, and said, 'Tomorrow at four o'clock we kill Germans.' "

"There were clocks?" I asked.

"They were Germans," Dov answered.

He was in the shoe repair shop at four o'clock. He picked up one of the steel forms they used to mend boots and smashed the German guard who was with him over the head. It had happened twenty years before, and he winced when he told it to me. "He was not a bad man," Dov said. And Dov ran for the fence.

He became part of a band of men who were looking for the Polish underground. They had rifles they'd taken from the Germans. And ammunition. And they found the Polish underground.

"Hand us your rifles and your bullets," they were told. "We'll give you food." They gave up their weapons and the Polish underground opened fire.

"As soon as I heard bullets, I ran," Dov told me.

There were two Polish undergrounds: the Communist underground, which had Jewish members, and the Royalist underground, which was as anti-Semitic as the Nazis.

Dov's gang dug two hideouts, about a mile apart, so they wouldn't all be found.

"One morning someone from the other group comes shouting, 'The Germans are here! The Germans are here!' They had followed him to our hideout. We had no guns, but someone looked in his pocket and found three bullets. There was a tunnel to get into our hideout, very small, big enough for one man. So, very loud — and in German so they would understand — we shouted, 'Pass me the rifle!' 'Let me have the pistol!' 'Give me the machine gun!' "

They held the bullets with sticks over a fire. It worked. When the bullets exploded from the heat, the German soldiers thought Dov's gang really did have guns. They ran away.

They found two Jews, brothers, farmers who had lived near Sobibor, hiding in the woods. "They couldn't read or write," Dov told me, a detail I remember. There was another member of their group, but I don't remember anything about him.

They all went to the brothers' farmhouse and saw smoke coming out of the chimney. Two Polish girls were living there. One had a German soldier's baby; the other was the sister of a leader of the Polish bandits. I had this image in my mind of what Polish bandits would look like, on horseback, knives held between their teeth, kerchiefs wrapped pirate fashion on the heads.

The three men kept the two women from turning them in, professing love, playing one against the other. Dov made it sound like a Feydeau farce. He, still a teenager and too young for the women, would inherit one of the largest fortunes in Lodz when the war was over, the women were told, and they would all be rich.

When the brother came to visit his sister, Dov joined his band and rode with the Polish bandits until the war was over.

"We drank a fifth of vodka a day to keep from freezing," Dov told me.

After the war, he went back to Lodz and didn't find anybody.

There is a documentary on the *Exodus* where you can see Dov on the ship's deck — small, curly hair. Someone is waving the Star of David, which would soon be used on the Israeli flag.

The real *Exodus* was turned back by the British; Sara and Dov and Dvaireh and Itzhak were interned in a British concentration camp on Cyprus, then sent back to a DP camp in Germany. When they did get to Israel, Dov told me, "There was a war. I got off the boat and they gave me a gun. Even though I was killing for my country, I wasn't" — he searched for the right word and knew he had to settle for one that wasn't a perfect translation. — "I wasn't . . . happy. I don't like killing."

Something happened in the years since the Holocaust. Then we were victims. Now we are survivors. It is all the difference in the world. I think it has something to do with the civil rights movement, with Martin Luther King and Malcolm X and black pride. In my own life, I am a cancer survivor; that's new, too. In the '50s and '60s, I would have been a victim of cancer, and it *is* all the difference in the world. Believe you're a survivor and your chest expands, you raise your shoulders, you stand up straight. Victims make themselves small and try to hide.

Yom ha-Shoah is a new Jewish holiday, the day we remember the Holocaust. Each year, Dov, something of a hero in Israel, is asked to represent the survivors in a national ceremony. I like to think he's asked not because he survived Sobibor, but that he's become a hero because he never learned to like killing.

<hr/>

It Helps to Have Captain America on Your Side

Stan Lee

Stan Lee, chairman of Marvel Comics and Marvel Films, created many legendary comic book characters, including Spider-Man, The Incredible Hulk, The X-Men, The Fantastic Four, Iron Man, Daredevil, and The Avengers. A member of the Signal Corps during World War II, he is one of only nine men in the United States Army to be given the military classification of "playwright."

My earliest recollection of growing up Jewish is my bar mitzvah in 1935. It's memorable because I had to undergo a crash course in Hebrew for a few days before the big event.

When I finally mastered the *"Baruch atah Adonai, Elohenu . . . ,"* I went to a little local temple in the Bronx with my father, who had been unemployed for years during the Depression. He had to grab a few other people who were in there praying at the time to come and bear witness to my entrance to manhood. So you see, it wasn't exactly the kind of spare-no-expense bar mitzvah you see in movies featuring suburban Jews.

Other than that, I've really not had many "Jewish experiences." Having lived in predominantly Jewish neighborhoods in Manhattan, then the Bronx, then Manhattan again, then Long Island, and now in racially mixed Los Angeles, I never experienced any prejudice that I can remember.

The only time it ever threatened to touch me was for a brief period in the army. When I was a sergeant, temporarily stationed at Fort Harrison in Indiana, there was a top kick who didn't relish the fact that I was Jewish. He seemed to feel that I was more of an enemy than the Nazis.

However, luckily for me, a fellow

noncom from rural Kentucky found out that I had written some Captain America comic books in my civilian life. He was a fanatical comic book fan. He was also the biggest, strongest human being imaginable — like Lenny in *Of Mice and Men*. This hulking backwoods giant became my biggest fan and virtual protector. Somehow or other, once it was known that "Kentucky" thought I was the greatest, the top kick apparently found some other Jewish GIs to harass because he never bothered me again.

Since then, I'm rarely reminded of my Jewish background except for the few times when I've been called on for interviews by writers for various Jewish newspapers and/or magazines. The subject they're interested in is usually the same: How come so many writers of superhero comic books are Jewish? Since I hate to disappoint them, I always try to come up with an answer but, in truth, I don't have the vaguest idea.

I'm glad to say, except for that brief experience in the army, I've rarely if ever encountered any memorable religious prejudice, probably because I've spent my whole career working with artists and writers and creative people of every race, color, and creed. In my experience, there's probably less religious prejudice in the artistic community than anywhere else.

Besides, my British wife is Episcopalian. "High Church of England," she calls it. Hey, who'd dare mess with the husband of someone like that!

PART III:

MILESTONES AND

HOLIDAYS

No matter how old you are, if you've had a bar or bat mitzvah, you remember it. When you're so old that your bones creak, you remember the pride you felt standing up there, knees knocking together, voice cracking at times, as you recited from the Torah in front of the entire congregation. You are now a man/you are now a woman. So how come, twenty years later when you go home for your Passover seder, they still seat you at the children's table? Which brings me to the seder table, another place of pungent memories. And from there to those Friday nights, and the lighting of the Shabbat candles. Of course, the High Holidays, Rosh Hashanah and Yom Kippur. Then there's Hanukkah (how *do* you spell that holiday, anyway?). Plus the one that we *don't* celebrate, Christmas. They're all here.

Boys don't remember their circumcision ceremony, the bris, normally performed on the eighth day after birth, but I've got a very unusual story for you here, from a Russian émigré, Dmitriy Salita, who didn't have it done as a baby but decided he wanted this mark of being a Jew for the rest of his life. That's true devotion, isn't it?

— Alan King

Melissa Manchester

Melissa Manchester began her career as a backup singer for Bette Midler and has gone on to record sixteen albums in two decades of performing. A winner of the Governor's Award from the National Academy of Recording Arts and Sciences, she crafted and also starred in Andrew Lloyd Webber's *Song and Dance* and *Music of the Night*, as well as Stephen Sondheim's musical *Sweeney Todd*.

What I remember most vividly about my Jewish upbringing was my mother lighting Friday night candles. I didn't know the whole family was supposed to gather around her. My sister and I were never encouraged to participate or learn the prayers. It was just the serene sight of my beautiful mother lighting the *Shabbos* candles that has always lingered in my memory.

My father, the atheist, made sure there was plenty of laughing during Passover seders, so of course I had no clue that seders were joyful, yet solemn, affairs. I thought they were a fabulous laughfest where the little ones were allowed, at age ten, to guzzle as much Mogen David as possible!

Decades later, I chose to have my own bat mitzvah. I embraced the core values of Judaism. And I am ever grateful that my parents let me find my way to the light.

> When I go to the synagogue today, there is a deep feeling that this is my heritage, this is my people. I am very much moved. It brings me back to the little boy who was bar mitzvahed.
>
> — Abe Vigoda

Bris

Dmitriy Salita

Dmitriy Salita is a young welterweight boxer and an observant Jew. When faced with Saturday matches, he has been known to say, "Anyone who wants a good whuppin' from me is just going to have to wait until sundown."

I came from Russia when I was nine years old. In Russia, even though I knew I was Jewish, we did not know about the Jewish customs and traditions. When I came here and my family became a bit more educated in Judaism, we decided it was time to get a bris. My goal was to do it before my bar mitzvah. I was eleven, one month away from my twelfth birthday, and the appointment was set up.

I was going to get circumcised.

Before going for the bris, I asked as many people as I knew about it, and of course my question was, "How much does it hurt?" The stories I got were not so bad. A lot of people told me they played soccer the next day, went for their final exam two days later, etc. *Doesn't sound so bad,* I thought.

Sometime in the afternoon we arrived at the private office somewhere in Brooklyn. I walked in and saw a table set up with cookies, wine, and a lot of other snacks. "What is this for?" I asked Boruch, who was the organizer of the event. "This is *L'chaim* to celebrate the occasion." *Looks good to me,* I thought. I proceeded into the waiting room. It was empty; there was one person ahead of me, and he was getting circumcised as I was waiting.

Five minutes went by . . . ten . . . fifteen . . . I started getting more and more nervous. My older brother, Mike, and my father tried to calm me down. Then it was my turn to go. As I was walking in, I saw an older man come into the office, dressed in traditional Jewish garb. "Who is this?" I asked Boruch. "He is here from France, a very big rabbi, and he came to support you in your task." I walked into the operating room, saw the scissors, saw the knife . . . and almost passed out.

I turned to everybody and said, "Guys, I don't think I can do it." Boruch and my family tried to calm me down and talk me into it, but it was not working. Boruch said, "This big rabbi is here just to see you get circumcised. He is a very big man and we don't get guests like this all the time." *It's not happening today,* I thought. They sent me back into the waiting room for ten minutes to think the situation over. *Maybe he will change his mind,* they thought.

Then Boruch asked my older brother, "Are you circumcised, Mike?"

"I am not," he answered.

"How about it, Mike?"

It did not take much convincing to get him going. He did it, and I felt like a weight had been lifted off my chest.

I was very grateful to my older brother.

I still had the goal of doing it before my bar mitzvah. I felt that it was an essential part of my life, to do it before I became a man. I did it when I was twelve, a month before my bar mitzvah.

It was not that bad, just mind over matter.

Jewish Christmas

Barbara Rushkoff

Barbara Rushkoff has been writing about Jews and pop culture since 1995, when she created *Plotz*, a self-published 'zine that has been transformed into a Web site, www.plotzworld.com. She is also the author of *Jewish Holiday Fun . . . For You*, a collection of irreverent retellings of Jewish holidays.

The summers of my youth were spent at La Coronado, a Jewish swim club with a Spanish name. La Coronado was mainly a bastion of ladies hanging out on the tip of the pool with cans of Tab and silver reflectors to get even more sun. It was there that I learned how to play mah-jongg and appreciate the aroma of coconut tanning oil mixed with menthol cigarettes. Most important, it's where I met the Taglian sisters.

Lisa and Maria Taglian didn't care that I was allergic to the sun and had big red sun spots, or that sometimes I wore a T-shirt over my bathing suit or that I had a cast on my wrist with a Baggie over it because I was also just a little bit slightly accident-prone. I didn't get why they hung out with me, because they were so glamorous with their dark tans, retail sandals, and gold lamé bikinis. I wore flip-flops from Korvettes, swimming costumes with little skirts attached, and nose plugs with my name written clearly on the strap. The Taglian girls were fancy. I liked that about them.

Their parents, Sy and Chandra Taglian, who took a shine to my parents, were also swanky. They had at least five hundred bucks on them at all times and much coinage, which they handed out freely. Our main activity at the dinner table was speculating loudly enough for the neighbors to hear about the origins of this money. Sy was a dry cleaner, although he never did divulge where his store was, nor did he seem to work much. And as nosy as my parents were, they never asked. Besides, it was much more fun to talk about it ad nauseam during dinner.

For some reason (free dry cleaning?) our

families bonded. And before you knew it, my Christmas fantasies were played out at their house as we were invited over to trim their tree. It was weird seeing the Taglians in clothing. I was so used to seeing major *toches* hanging out of damp bathing suits and chlorine-crusted feet that when we entered their house and they were dressed in Bill Cosby–like sweaters, it took me a minute to adjust.

We didn't believe in Christmas at our house, but in other people's homes it was just fine. We were led into the living room, where a plastic Jesus was the centerpiece. He looked to be wearing a tinsel prom dress. Again, fancy. Also, mixed drinks called highballs were waiting for every single one of us. My parents let us drink them to calm down our frenzied decorating style (which was throwing tinsel on anything that moved). Talk about classy. And tasty, too!

We never had liquor in our house. Sure, we had a black-and-white bar with cute matching stools in our Colonial furnished rec room that held little bottles of Old Grand Dad and liqueurs with names like Cherry-Chocolate and Orange-Something-Something. But there was never wine with dinner, no late-night cocktails, no nothing.

I thought that Jews didn't drink. They drugged, all right, but they didn't drink. Who would want to drink that stuff anyway — Mogen David? We had a pill for everything in our house. It was okay. The doctor said so. Take one? How about taking ten? That worked better. Drinking was for the other religions.

Christmas at the Taglians' was fun. In between desecrating the tree with way too much clumped tinsel and drinking festive mugs of holiday whiskey, I liked to zone out at the nativity spot. That was quite a scene — wise men, a newborn baby, and a virgin bride. What a story line! It made me feel a little ripped off, though. Hanukkah had nothing juicy like this attached to it. Lighting candles and saying blessings in Hebrew with a Philadelphia accent is not exactly the same thing. Where's *our* cute li'l baby Jesus to dress up in a cotton ball pantsuit?

Also, every other non-Jewish kid I knew was getting a ton of presents all at the same time. And they were all better than mine. Mittens and gym shorts did not a happy Hanukkah make. (Oh, wow. Under-shirts. Thanks.) But the Taglians would give us totally useless presents that we loved: hot pink jewelry boxes with bubble rings in them, suede chokers with the eternal sign for peace on them, and nail polish in colors that we weren't allowed to wear. Besides bringing them some home-made *mandel* bread, my parents "thanked" the Taglians for their generosity by inviting them to our house for Passover. Now, it's one thing to do this with your own family with no outsiders at the table, and so when my parents got the bright idea that we should invite the Taglians, I knew it was a mistake. You see, my extended family doesn't exactly get along with each other. Or anyone else!

My dad's parents were nice people who smelled like mothballs, red meat, and teeth. We called them Bubbe and Zaideh. My mother's parents were a little more hip. They liked to be called Nanny and Pop-Pop. We liked them a little better because they gave us money. Nanny even taught us a little trick about drinking the Passover wine. Instead of taking a sip, she would tell us to down the whole cup. She would be drunk almost immediately, giggling at the lamb shank and making jokes about "hiding the matzo." I enjoyed this very much, but it would incense my father, who'd give Nanny an extra dose of horse-radish on her gefilte fish. It kind of tied into the holiday, as we'd reinforce the theme of punishing the Jews right at our seder table. Who said that Jewish holidays aren't fun?

As Nanny got drunker and Dad got angrier, I wondered what the Taglians thought. Were they horrified? Repelled? Appalled? Jealous? Bloated? We didn't know because after the seder we never heard from them again. *Ever.* When we called, they didn't answer. When we drove by their house, it was boarded up. Gosh, were we that awful that they felt they had to leave the immediate area? When summer came, they didn't join the swim club, either. What? Was it something we said?

Of course that meant that there would be no Jewish Christmas for us that year. There would be no tinsel time, no dressing up Jesus, and no more delicious hooch. We all took it pretty hard until we found out that Mr. Taglian had been arrested for fronting stolen goods at his dry-cleaning store. I heard words like "repossessed" and "foreclosure" at the dinner table. It was sad, but honestly it was a relief to hear that our Passover seder wasn't the culprit that had distanced them from us. It was just good, old-fashioned crime! Whew.

I think about the Taglians every Christmas as I wistfully light my menorah. I've learned over the years that Hanukkah isn't as lame as I thought it was. We get to play with fire, and that is a little cooler than throwing tinsel on a tree. And as I stare into the flames, I think about that. Then I immediately start craving a highball. Here's to you, Taglians, wherever you are.

❧

Matzo Balls and Me

Lesléa Newman

Lesléa Newman is the author of *Heather Has Two Mommies*. She has received the James Baldwin Award for Cultural Achievement, two Pushcart Prize nominations, and the *Highlights for Children* Fiction Writing Award.

When I want to revisit my Jewish childhood, I don't have to go very far. All I have to do is glance at a small framed photo on my desk, and I am home. The photo shows a beautiful woman with curly auburn hair, delicate gold hoops in her ears, and a knowing look in her eye. The woman is my grandmother, Ruth

Levin, and the photo was taken when she was ninety-nine years old.

My grandmother was born in 1890 and came to this country when she was ten. "What day is your birthday, Grandma?" I asked her more than once.

"I don't know." She'd shrug. "Sometime around Passover."

"Where were you born, Grandma?"

Again the shrug. "Sometimes they called it Poland, sometimes they'd call it Russia. Have some applesauce, *mamela,* and stop with the questions."

I grew up in Brighton Beach, in a neighborhood filled with Jews "from the old country." My grandmother, who was like a third parent to me, lived across the street. When I was eight years old, my family made aliyah to Long Island. I missed my grandmother terribly. When she came to visit, she slept on the spare bed in my room, displacing my beloved Cairn terrier, Angus, whom she called Agnes. My grandmother visited frequently, and of course she always came for Passover.

No seder would ever be complete without my grandmother's famous matzo ball soup. I'd ask her how many carrots to put in, how much celery. "Enough," was her stock reply.

"But how do you know how much is enough?" I'd press her.

"When you're old enough to know, you'll know," she'd say, adding a *bissl* salt.

Though we weren't allowed to eat the Passover meal until we had arrived at the proper place in the Haggadah, different members of my family always found an excuse to visit the kitchen to "check on something." What we were all really doing was sneaking bites of my grandmother's soup. Later, as an adult, I immortalized this family tradition in a children's book called *Matzo Ball Moon*. In the story, so many family members sneak off to steal a matzo ball, that when it's time actually to serve the soup, there aren't enough matzo balls for everyone. The grandmother in the story, just like my own grandmother, puts her family before herself and goes without. But when her young granddaughter opens the door for Elijah the Prophet, she sees the full moon and thinks that it is "so big and lumpy and bumpy, it looks just like a matzo ball." With great excitement, she tells her grandmother she has found a special matzo ball just for her. When the girl's beloved *bubbe* joins her at the front door, the girl presents her with the "big, bumpy, lumpy, yummy-looking matzo ball moon."

When my grandmother died, one of the things I inherited was her soup pot. The first time I made matzo ball soup in it, I put the matzo balls right in with the chicken and the carrots and the celery and the parsley and the dill. An hour later, I checked on the soup. To my horror, it was gone, soaked up by the matzo balls as though they were sponges. The next time I made it, I had better luck. Somehow, as if I were a sponge myself, I absorbed what I needed to know all those years watching my grandmother make her soup.

Nowadays, my matzo ball soup is a Passover seder staple. And for some reason, various members of my family always find a reason to sneak into the kitchen to "check on things" as we make our way through the Haggadah. And I could swear there are always fewer matzo balls when I serve the soup than there were when I made it. But somehow, there are always enough.

Don Rickles

Don Rickles has appeared on countless television shows and in *Kelly's Heroes*, with Clint Eastwood; *Casino*, with Robert De Niro; and *Toy Story*, with Tom Hanks.

When I was thirty-nine, a memorable moment occurred that reminded me about my faith. The night before my wedding, my cousin and I were staying at a hotel. At five p.m., my cantor, who knew me a lifetime, called me and said, "Get dressed and come down." He drove us out to Elmont Cemetery, where my father was buried. The cantor stood by the grave and sang a prayer inviting my father to the wedding. It was a beautiful and touching moment that I'll never forget.

The Nuns' Seder

Sally J. Priesand

Sally J. Priesand is America's first female rabbi. She is the author of *Judaism
and the New Woman* and has been featured in *Rabbis: The Many Faces of Judaism* and *Fifty Jewish Women Who
Changed the World.*

I grew up in Cleveland, a city that has one of
the largest and most active Jewish communities in the country. Nonetheless, living as we
did in the western suburbs, my brothers and
I were the only Jews in our high school. As a
result, many of our closest friends were those
we made in youth group and religious
school, which in our synagogue (Beth Israel
— The West Temple) continued through the
twelfth grade. My family was very active in

temple activities, and my parents gave willingly of themselves to support the programs and projects of our congregation, whether through positions of leadership or simply as volunteers. On Friday nights, we were always the last ones to leave, having helped clean up after the *oneg Shabbat* (which more often than not included something my mother had baked — her culinary skills were, and are, a source of wonder and delight in our congregation).

I have many fond memories of growing up Jewish in a non-Jewish neighborhood. Passover was especially festive in our house. Each year, my siblings and I invited non-Jewish friends to share seder with us. I can still see my father at the head of our table, reclining on his pillow, leaving the table at the appropriate time to wash his hands, explaining the symbols on the seder plate and reading every word of the Haggadah. My mother, of course, had been preparing for days, making gefilte fish from scratch and fashioning those delicious matzo balls that were especially light and fluffy.

One year, my father's business brought him into contact with a Catholic children's home run by a group of nuns. Passover was approaching, and in the course of conversation, the mother superior began asking questions about the customs and traditions of this holiday. Before long, my father had offered to conduct a seder for fifty-two nuns (and the monsignor!), volunteering my mother, of course, to oversee the meal and make enough chicken soup and matzo balls for all the participants. My father read the Haggadah, and the youngest nun recited the Four Questions. My mother still remembers entering the dining room on the day of the seder and being greeted by a huge sign that simply said SHALOM. Moreover, the nuns presented her with a beautiful two-tiered silver tray that we continue to cherish.

My father died in 1968. I will never forget the kindness of the nuns, who, dressed in their traditional garb, came to our home while we were sitting shiva to remember my father and give thanks for his life. And I am ever grateful to my parents for teaching us by example that all people are God's children, and we have much to learn from each other.

Leslie Epstein

Leslie Epstein has written nine novels, including *King of the Jews* and *San Remo Drive: A Novel from Memory*. He grew up in Los Angeles, where his father, Julius Epstein, was a screenwriter and coauthor, with his uncle Philip, of the classic films *Casablanca, Arsenic and Old Lace*, and *Yankee Doodle Dandy*.

I was born in Los Angeles one year before the Germans invaded Poland, which means that I was three and a half years old when America entered World War Two. For me, in knee pants and on the sidelines, the war was essentially a matter of Japan and Japanese. The paper drives at Brentwood Elementary, the bacon grease stored in tin cans, the brown barrage balloons tied off Santa Monica Pier: all this — not to mention the disappearance of certain classmates, along with the old gentleman who smoothed our garden with his bamboo rake — was directed at the nation that had attacked us with such treachery at Pearl Harbor and that, rumor had it, dropped parachute bombs upon Seattle and lurked off our coast

199

in submarines. About the war in Europe, I knew little or nothing.

Not coincidentally, Judaism and Jews were as absent from my childhood as Germany and its crimes. Neither I nor my brother, Ricky, was bar mitzvahed. We never went to temple. Indeed, I doubt I heard the words "Rosh Hashanah" or "Yom Kippur" until I was well out of my teens. We lived, just after the war, in a part of Pacific Palisades where even the movie people — Gregory Peck up the street, Virginia Bruce and Linda Darnell a block away, Joseph Cotten kitty-corner, and Robert Mitchum on the school bus route down Mandeville Canyon — were unlikely to dwell upon the Day of Atonement.

Needless to say, then, we celebrated Christmas and did not know the word "Hanukkah," much less what it stood for. Instead we put up trees, giant firs and spruces, whose stars — emblematic of the supernova over Bethlehem — grazed our twelve-foot ceilings. There were red balls and silver cataracts of tinsel and galaxies of winking lights — all strung by the black maid and butler the previous night. Mary and Arthur were there the next morning, too: she to receive her woolen sweater; he, his briar pipe. Of course, my brother and I were frantic with greed, whipped up by weeks of unintelligible hymns (*myrrh,* for instance, or *roundyon* from "Silent Night," or the Three Kings' *orientare*), the mesmerizing lights, the smell of the tree itself, and the sea of packages beneath it — and perhaps above all by the prospect of that rarest of all Epstein family phenomena: the sight of our parents, in dressing gowns, with coffee cups, downstairs before the UCLA chimes struck noon.

To a child, and not just a child, the trappings of a Christmas must trump any other holiday. Think, for example, of the yearly pageant within the public schools of California. I played a bearded shepherd one year, the rear end of a cow the next. How could the meager detritus of Hanukkah — a few flimsy candles, a horde of chocolate coins, an incomprehensible prayer — compete with that bright star in the heavens, the wise men and their gifts, and the sweet animals gathered around the little halo-headed fellow before whom all had dropped to their knees?

Not only had I no knowledge of the Festival of Lights or the other Jewish holidays, I doubt that for the first decade of my life I even heard the word "Jew." To some degree this vacancy was not atypical. My parents, the son and daughter of Yiddish-speaking immigrants, like many of the emancipated second generation, were hell-bent on sparing the third the kind of Orthodox regime they had had to undergo themselves. What *was* atypical, and decisive, was the position my father and uncle (together they wrote *Arsenic and Old Lace, The Man Who Came to Dinner, The Strawberry Blonde, Yankee Doodle Dandy, Casablanca,* and dozens more) held in the film industry. It is no secret that by the mid-thirties, when Phil and Julie arrived in Hollywood, the men who ran the studios had decided upon their own policy of ethnic cleansing. You can see the process in the descending generations of *Abie's Irish Rose* (the bearded, accented grandparents, then the assimilated and intermarried Abie and Rosemary, and finally the genetic miracle: a lass, Rebecca, and Patrick, the lad) and in what the critic Patricia Erens calls "the tradition of casting Jewish actors as parents and Gentile-looking actors as their children." What roles, then, could Ricky and I play? If the "Epstein boys" were busily creating the American dream in, say, *Yankee Doodle Dandy,* their children had little choice but to join that great national audience of white, upturned, anonymous faces. Or think of it this way: If the words "Jewish" and "Jew" disappeared from every American film for the whole of World War Two (with the sole exception, it pleases me to say, of Julie and Phil's *Mr. Skeffington*), is it surprising that they might also vanish from the households of those engaged upon American culture's front lines?

What needs to be explained, then, was how as an adolescent at University High I could write a story about a crowd milling through a plaza in South America, a crowd which — to make a bad story short — begins to cry out to the lone, mustachioed figure on a palace balcony, "Viva! Viva Hitler!" From where, in my sheltered and rather Aryanized life, had this vision of evil come? Oh, I had had plenty of hints in conversations around the dinner table, had eventually seen the photographs in *Life* of bulldozers at work on small mountains of bodies and the other photos of the ovens, the showers, the ditches. But I believe the truth is that for all the machinations of Hollywood and its masters and even the larger culture and whatever the proclivities of my own psyche, I had always known — in the same way that one knows from childhood the laws of gravity. What goes up must come down. From childhood? I might have been born with an innate grasp of the fate of the Jews. What a person learns, later, the facts of physics, the formulas about the mass of objects and the square of their distance, only confirms what he carries within like the weight of his bones. Hints, hushings, inflections, a glance — these pass from Jew to Jew, and from child to child, by a kind of psychic osmosis. So it was that history passed molecule by molecule through the membrane that held me apart from my fellows and apart from a world long denied.

If we flash-forward to any December of the last two or even three decades, you might well find me lighting a candle and handing it to one of my three children, while I mumble, or mouth, the words of a phonetic prayer. For a time there were Christmas trees, but the taller my daughter and her twin brothers grew, the more the greenery shrank. The pull of the Christian holiday, which I had thought invincible — those carols and crèches, Santas and sanctimony — did not seem all that attractive to the kids. At one point my daughter's boyfriend refused to come up from New York because we still had a sixteen-inch construction of twigs with cotton snow from various pill bottles stretched out underneath. For the last few years we've had nothing but gelt in various flavors and denominations, along with a plaster menorah that brightens up on each of the eight evenings in an attempt to duplicate the miracle of the original light. Probably, now that that daughter has married another Jewish boy and provided us with a grandchild, I'll end up spinning a dreidel in my dotage.

Not that anyone in the family is a fanatic. When I proposed to the boys that they might want to attend Sunday school in preparation for a bar mitzvah that I had never had myself, they hooted at my hypocrisy, and I settled for having them read *This Way to the Gas, Ladies and Gentlemen* and John Hersey's *The Wall*. And I don't think my daughter, weddings and funerals aside, has spent a single day in a temple. Yet each of them is able to recite the appropriate blessing without the help of a crib sheet and thinks of himself or herself, when they think of such matters at all, as a Jew.

As for me, after that first short story set in Buenos Aires, every one of my novels implicitly or explicitly has dealt with the tragedy of the Jews. Not that my work or my experience of life would make a rabbi proud. I turned to a consciousness of my race for two reasons: first, because of the Holocaust. I think that on some level of consciousness I decided that if a cruel world from Haman to Hitler had tried to exterminate my people, then I was not going to let America, through kindness and assimilation, complete the task. Second, my upbringing. In men, as in nature, a vacuum must be filled. If I had grown up in another, less sunny, city, or outside the shadow of its dominant industry, or to other parents in other times — that is, if I had come into maturity as either a Jewish believer or simply a Jewish child, what I subsequently learned about the fate of the Jews themselves would not have exerted sufficient force to draw me into the orbit of the ancient and unhappy people, about which I must now forever revolve.

> There are some Jews in this town [Hollywood] and nobody knows about it. But we really like being Jewish. You don't have to see a bullfrog to hear him croak.
>
> — Aaron Spelling

High Holidays in the Granite State

Daniel Mariaschin

Daniel Mariaschin has spent nearly all of his adult life working on behalf of Jewish organizations, including the Anti-Defamation League and the American Zionist Federation. He has participated in meetings with world leaders, including Margaret Thatcher, Helmut Kohl, King Hussein of Jordan, Czech president Vaclav Havel, Moroccan King Hassan II, Lech Walesa, and Eduard Shevardnadze.

In 1955, just before I entered the first grade, our family moved from New Jersey to Swanzey, New Hampshire. Our town (population two thousand five hundred) had only three Jewish families, but Keene — the closest city (and where my parents had

207

bought a women's clothing store) — had a small synagogue serving the twenty-five families who lived within a twenty-five-mile radius.

The shul was a converted stately old home near the center of the tree-lined town, which was known as "the Elm City." Its sanctuary seated about eighty persons, and there was a small Hebrew school classroom and a tiny social hall used for the occasional kiddush or special meeting. Our rabbis — and we had several over a short period of time — lived upstairs in a large apartment.

Near the entrance of the sanctuary was a large sitting room, comfortably furnished with sofas and lined with tall bookcases. It was here that the synagogue's board met and where other important business was conducted.

On the High Holidays, it became the place to take a break from the services. Invariably, Rosh Hashanah and Yom Kippur coincided with the onset of Indian summer, when the sanctuary's windows were opened — in that pre-air-conditioned era — to let in some air. Holiday time also meant a bigger crowd than normal at services; folding chairs were added outside the sanctuary to accommodate the overflow of children, grandchildren, and other relatives who came home for the *chag*.

My father, who after retirement became the community's Hebrew school teacher, was a religious man who arrived early and stayed late for services. I came with him and sat next to him in the fourth or fifth row in the sanctuary. We sat behind Abe Fine, the furrier, and next to Keever Chorney, an older man who always davened at his own pace — and superfast, I thought. I can still hear the sweet voice of Meyer "Mike" Goldman, a pharmacist from nearby Peterborough, who served as hazan each year.

When you are nine or ten years old, the tendency in such circumstances is to sit for a while and then leave on some pretext in order to join the other kids who had the same idea. There wasn't a "junior congregation" or children's service to keep us occupied. If the weather was good, sometimes we'd go out and play on the lawn in front of the shul. Usually, though, we repaired to the sitting room, which was large enough to accommodate us and the adults who were taking their own break. Mostly, we'd jabber, as kids do, about all manner of things. I recall the good-hearted Jerry Weinrieb, circling the room on Yom

Kippur, offering smelling salts to those adults who were beginning to feel light-headed from the fast.

It was in the sitting room that I became a Yankees fan. The High Holidays then, as now, coincided with the end of baseball season and the beginning of the World Series. The talk among the men usually centered on the pennant races or, depending on the calendar, the series itself. I listened carefully to the chatter but paid most attention to Freddie Klein, who operated a commercial glass shop, talk up the Yankees. The Yanks were in the series every year in those days (like today) and had all those powerful lineups. Despite our being in Red Sox country, Freddie made the Yankees bigger than life for me, and if they were good enough to be his team, that was good enough for me, too.

It wasn't long before my father would come looking for me, and it was clear that I'd better go back and join him inside. I knew it must be important for him that I return to services.

As I look back, sitting next to him is my best memory of those days. He davened with such *kavanah* — devotion — that I surmised, in my ten-year-old mind — that this was the most important thing one could possibly do. I often lost my place, and he would pause, without missing any of the prayers himself, and point to the place in the siddur where we were in the service. Without telling me, he conveyed respect for the whole notion of prayer.

Little did I know that his example would serve me for a lifetime.

<hr/>

Menorah

Ruth Laredo

Ruth Laredo, a three-time Grammy Award nominee, has performed at Carnegie Hall, Lincoln Center, Kennedy Center, and the White House, and with the New York Philharmonic, Philadelphia Orchestra, and Boston Symphony. She has also served as special arts correspondent for National Public Radio's *Morning Edition*.

According to family tradition, my maternal grandfather, Adolph Horowitz, had once been a pattern maker for the queen of Romania. All I knew, as a child growing up in Detroit, was that my grandpa made holiday dreidels for his grandchildren and that he was the creator and designer of the extraordinarily beautiful menorah that graced the mantel in our living room. We used it for family candle-lighting ceremonies at Shabbat and Hanukkah.

Very few such menorahs were ever produced: I have one in my New York apartment, and my sister, Rayna Kogan, another in her home in West Bloomfield, Michigan.

Little did I know that this menorah would eventually become a prized work of art — the very same menorah with the two proud lions, one on each side of the Ten Commandments spelled out in Hebrew letters of brass.

Just such a menorah turned up in the art gallery of Temple Beth El in Detroit many years after my grandfather died. I was in Detroit to perform in some concerts for the Great Lakes Chamber Music Festival, which uses the chapel of the temple as one of its performance spaces.

En route to a rehearsal within the temple, I was astonished to discover an exhibit of Hebrew artifacts displayed in the art gallery. There, among the great and beautiful ancient and modern menorahs was one that my grandfather had made so many years ago, the one that had belonged to my parents and that had been so much a part of my childhood. I do not know how it happened to be there — but what a wonderful surprise and enduring reminder of the artistry of my grandfather!

⟡⟡⟡⟡⟡

A Stormy Bar Mitzvah

Larry Brown

Larry Brown is head coach of the Detroit Pistons. A recipient of numerous awards, Brown has coached basketball at the collegiate and professional level for more than thirty years.

I grew up in Long Beach, Long Island, on top of my grandfather's bakery, Hittleman's, where my entire family worked. I lost my father when I was young, and my mother and the rest of the family helped raise me. Across the street from the bakery was the neighborhood playground attached to Central School. When I came home from school, I played ball there until my mother blinked the lights to signal that it was time for me to go home. I attended Hebrew school reluctantly, as it interfered with the only thing I wanted to do — play ball.

When the time drew near for my bar mitzvah, my mother arranged for me to take Hebrew lessons at Rabbi Solomon's house, just six doors down from the playground. If I had a three to four p.m. lesson, I would conveniently be late or, in some cases, Rabbi Solomon would drag me off the court by my ear. As much as I resisted, I had to have Hebrew lessons to prepare for my bar mitzvah.

Rabbi Solomon was a great rabbi. He took pride in the fact that all boys who studied under him did well. But with me, it was a different story. He repeatedly became frustrated with me and told me how bad I was making him look. He thought I would ruin his reputation or embarrass him with my poor Hebrew skills. On the Friday before my bar mitzvah, Rabbi Solomon took me for my rehearsal, and I did horribly. I knew nothing! I went blank. Rabbi Solomon was in a state of flux. He told my mom that I could not go on with the ceremony, that I would embarrass myself, my family, and the rabbi himself. But all day Friday, my mom stayed up with me and helped me prepare. Later that night, a hurricane swept through our neighborhood. My mother told me it was an omen. "This is what happens when you don't study," she warned me. The storm calmed down enough for me to go on with the ceremony. I somehow managed to remember everything I had been taught in those Hebrew lessons; it was almost like a message from God. I looked over at Rabbi Solomon, and he was as white as a ghost; he could not believe that I got through it. So although I would rather have been out playing ball than inside learning Hebrew, my bar mitzvah went well, and I did not embarrass Rabbi Solomon after all.

A synagogue was infested with rats. The rabbi called in an exterminator, who said he'd get rid of them, but a week later, the rats were back. The rabbi had the exterminator in again, but a month later, the rats were back. He called in the exterminator for the third time, but this time the exterminator said, "I don't think I can help you. These are very stubborn rats." The rabbi was about to give up, when suddenly an idea came to him. "I know!" he said. "I'll just bar mitzvah them all, and then they'll never return!"

— Old Joke

Warner Wolf

Warner Wolf is the three-time Sports-
caster of the Year who coined the catch-
phrase "Let's go to the videotape!" Wolf
was bar mitzvahed in 1986, at the age
of forty-eight.

I was born on November 11, 1937 (then
called Armistice Day), an only child, to Jack
and Rosemary Wolf in Washington, DC. In
fact, my father was born on July 4, my
mother on Labor Day. They were married
on Thanksgiving, and one of my daughters,
Shayna, was born on Memorial Day.

My first introduction to Judaism came at
an early age. Al Jolson's father, who was a
mohel in Washington, did my bris.

My parents were vaudevillians and told
me many stories about their travels. They
played all the big-time theaters including
the Palace in New York City and the Palla-
dium in London. My parents were married
in Chicago, shortly after my mother converted to Judaism. The funny thing is, she
became more Jewish than anyone else. One
time in college, I brought this terrific girl

home to dinner. My mother didn't care for her because she wasn't Jewish. "You brought home a shiksa?" she asked.

The thing I remember most about growing up in a Jewish home was that during the High Holidays, my mother and father, my aunt and uncle, and their two children always celebrated at my grandfather and grandmother's house — Rose and Charlie Wolf. And without fail, as if on cue, every single time, when my grandfather would go to make a toast, he would look at the seven of us (not counting his wife) and start crying. He could never get the words out. Every year, the same time, the same thing. I never understood this until I had my own family.

For some reason, I was never bar mitzvahed as a thirteen-year old.

I went to the Washington Hebrew Congregation, one of the oldest Reform synagogues in the country, and we were all members of the 1954 confirmation class, presided over by the legendary Rabbi Norman Gerstenfeld.

But the fact that I wasn't bar mitzvahed still bothered me as I grew older. I kept it to myself and never mentioned it to anyone.

Both my parents died at an early age —

my father at fifty-six and my mother seven years later, at fifty-eight. Then one day I picked up the paper and read that eighty-year-old Henny Youngman, who also had never been bar mitzvahed, was having a bar mitzvah in Atlantic City. If Henny Youngman could do it at eighty, it wasn't too late for me. So for one solid year, Cantor Seymour Schwarzmer of Mount Vernon, New York, came to my house every Tuesday at eleven a.m. He prepared me for my bar mitzvah, mostly in Hebrew, and I wanted to chant, rather than read. The learning experience was terrific. One year later, on June 21, 1986, at age forty-eight, Warner William Wolf became a bar mitzvah boy.

One of my oldest friends, Lew Citren, gave a little blessing and said, "Warner, you were at my bar mitzvah thirty-five years ago; it took you a long time to recip-rocate."

What was my motivating force? I felt I didn't want to break the tradition in my family.

Another great Jewish experience oc-curred when I was voted into the Wash-ington, DC, Jewish Sports Hall of Fame in 1993, along with Red Auerbach, and in 1999 into the New York Jewish Sports Hall of Fame, going in with former pitcher Kenny Holtzman and the great boxing manager and trainer Ray Arcel.

However, my most meaningful Jewish story occurred on January 24, 1991. I flew to Israel during the Gulf War. I have never had a feeling in my heart as I did on this occasion. I wanted to be there to lend my support the best I could. I called a friend of mine on Israeli TV, Menashe Raz, and asked him if there was anything I could do. He said, "Yes, and bring your videotapes." Because of the war and the scud missiles, no one was going out and everyone was staying home, watching TV. I got permission to leave the station from my boss, Roger Colloff.

I went. I was on Israeli TV morning, afternoon, and night with my plays of the year, plays of the month. They even piped in the Giants Bills Super Bowl, video only, no sound. I did the analysis in English, and Yuri Levy did the play-by-play in Hebrew. I didn't know what he was saying, but he knew what I was saying. After pointing out that the Giants held the ball for 9.5 minutes and kept their defense off the field, Yuri said, "I just said that in Hebrew." After the broadcast, Menashe said to me, "Warner, you had a captive audience and you were on coast to coast." Not bad, until you realize that Israel is only the size of New Jersey.

The next day I was taking a taxi from Jerusalem to Tel Aviv. The cabdriver turned around and asked me if I was an actor. I told him I had just been on Israeli TV. He became very excited and called his brother on the phone. He asked me to talk to his brother, who was also excited to talk to me. Apparently, I was big in Israel. We picked up an Israeli soldier hitchhiking. He kept looking at me. The cabdriver told him who I was. *He* became excited. He said I gave the soldiers in the barracks some entertainment and took their minds off the war.

I felt, if I ever had a purpose in life, maybe that was it.

<hr/>

A Yom Kippur Remembrance

Melvin Jules Bukiet

Melvin Jules Bukiet's most recent books are *Strange Fire*, a novel, *A Faker's Dozen*, a collection, and *Nothing Makes You Free: Writings by Descendants of Jewish Holocaust Survivors*, an anthology. He teaches at Sarah Lawrence College.

The Bronx, 1966. My parents are preparing a grand Rosh Hashanah dinner for several hundred relatives — at least it seems that way to my five-year-old eyes. Unfortunately those same eyes as well as my nose poking into the pots on the stove and especially my fingers are in the way, so I'm sent off on an entirely superfluous and glorious errand to a local candy store to buy several pounds of chocolate for after-dinner treats.

The candy store is a cornucopia of goodies, freshly made in an aromatic back room by Mr. and Mrs. Bernstein, the proprietors. I've known the Bernsteins for practically as long as I've known my mother and father. She's a bit of a scold, but he slips me "samples" before I purchase a carefully chosen selection of chocolates, some with coconut shavings, some with a hazelnut cream center, some with raspberry filling.

Of course, I see the Bernsteins in shul the next day and I see them ten days later during Yom Kippur services, when Mr. Bernstein winks at me and says, "No chocolate today."

Trying to fast, lasting as long as lunch, I

nod somberly and vow that my lunch will be a dry crust rather than any of Mr. Bernstein's delights.

I never see Mr. Bernstein again, however, because he's murdered the next day. All we know is that a "hoodlum" forced his way into the store when Mr. Bernstein was alone, tied him up and duct-taped his mouth, and stole the receipts from the cash register. Bernstein suffocated.

At Hebrew school later that week, I ask the rabbi why this happened.

The rabbi answered, "Mr. Bernstein was a lucky man. By dying on the day after Yom Kippur, all of his sins were cleansed."

Lucky.

I still can't hear the word without thinking of Mr. Bernstein, and I've never since then even tried to fast on Yom Kippur. Instead, I eat chocolate.

I once wanted to become an atheist but I gave up — they have no holidays.
— Henny Youngman

The Night My Father
Invented Champagne

Melville Shavelson

Melville Shavelson's films include *The Seven Little Foys* and *Houseboat*. He is also the author of *How to Make a Jewish Movie* and has served as president of the Writers Guild of America.

I remember it was 1930, because that was the time the cows had their hooves sticking up in the air and I became bar mitzvahed. It was a happy time for me and the Holsteins. The cows had their moment first. I was crossing the pasture that was a shortcut to our house when I saw them lying in the lush grass, on their backs, hooves waving in the air. I ran to tell my father — it was Sunday, the store in Spring Valley, New York, was closed. Our house, by the way, was located almost exactly on the state line separating New York from New Jersey, a crucial point, although I didn't realize it until later.

Dad took one look at the cows and ran into the house to get a huge glass jar we kept in the cellar for making pickles. His fondest hopes had been confirmed.

The farm next door had been sold to a

mysterious family some months earlier. We saw them occasionally, a family consisting entirely of hard-faced Italian men who didn't seem to know too much about the cows that were kept in their huge red barn. A lot of workmen had been occupied in that barn for weeks; we never could figure out why. Certainly cows didn't require indoor plumbing, but from all the pipes and boilers being delivered at night, they could have been building a bovine replica of the ladies' room at Radio City Music Hall.

The compost pile outside the barn took on a pungent aroma. The cows' condition immediately confirmed my father's suspicion: The compost was no longer compost; it was mash, the residue of a huge distilling operation, which the cows had obviously been feasting upon and had begun dancing in the meadow, vine leaves figuratively in their hair, drunk as skunks and happy as larks.

For my father, it was a religious experience. Prohibition had made it difficult for him to worship God in the manner God demanded at Passover. The sacramental wine that was an integral part of that holiday was almost impossible to obtain and tremendously expensive. The usual vintage, which we referred to as Manischewitz Holy Water, was now illegal. Since near our home there was an abundant supply of chokecherries and elderberries, my father had considered it his religious duty to make the wine to supply the relatives in Brooklyn every year, so that the Exodus from Egypt and the parting of the Red Sea could be properly celebrated with the traditional biblical hangovers. But Dad's wine never quite compared with Mouton Rothschild '27, although, as the relatives were quick to point out, Baron Rothschild was equally Jewish. He must have gone to temple more often than my father.

In our family, the Hebrew prayer for wine was usually accompanied by an invocation for a rapid recovery from drinking Château Shavelson '30.

Dad kept trying. Every summer, we children would be put to picking baskets of the tiny black chokecherries from the trees that lined our driveway. Dad would carefully put the cherries down in oaken barrels in the cellar, a layer of sugar, a layer of cherries, and so forth. Then he would cork the barrels and let nature take its course.

Within a month, without fail, the result was twenty gallons of Château Shavelson vinegar.

Since the Bible doesn't mention much about drinking holy vinegar, obviously something had to be done. Every year, the Chanins in Brooklyn would send out the patriarch of their family. We called him Zaideh, although he really wasn't our grandfather. But he *looked* like a Zaideh. He was a dignified old man with crisp blue eyes and a manicured white beard, always dressed in a black frock coat and carrying a brown valise and a Malacca cane. He would step off the Erie Railroad train at our little station like the Messiah himself — I secretly believed he *was,* and I had a sneaking suspicion *he* did, too — and climb into the Chevrolet delivery truck beside my father and me for the trip home.

Once in the house, he would put on his prayer shawl and his tefillin and pray mysteriously to his God for help. After all, if Jesus could turn water into wine, couldn't Jehovah turn vinegar into Mouton Rothschild?

Having finished his prayers, Zaideh would then repair to our basement, open his brown valise, and take out the most complete and compact still I have ever seen, one he had manufactured himself to precise tolerance so it would fit in the valise and leave room for several gallon jars of the finished product. It included a series of Pyrex glass retorts, tubes, and Bunsen burners designed to distill the product in my father's wine barrels into the high-powered, one-hundred-proof schnapps the Lord really preferred to Manischewitz. The trick was to catch the wine in the barrels just before it transformed itself into salad dressing.

Science always met its match in Château Shavelson wine. The timing was never quite right. All the still ever produced was schnapps vinegar, if there is such a thing. It would take the lining off a stomach without achieving any of the agreeable side effects so apparent in the cows later to be found cavorting in the nearby meadow. After a day or two of fruitless distilling, Zaideh would sadly pack his paraphernalia, fill a gallon jar with the awful results just to show the relatives what a schlemiel my father was as a winemaker, and depart hastily on the Erie Railroad — shouting an occasional epithet in Hebrew — for the thirsty, religious throng waiting in Brooklyn.

That is why my father leaped immediately into action when I told him about the cows next door. He carried the huge glass pickle jar over to the neighbors' house with me tagging along and immediately borrowed a gallon of pure grain alcohol, two hundred proof. No vinegar in the world could resist this additive. The relatives would learn soon enough who was the real Baron Rothschild!

Until this moment, we hadn't met our neighbors, but Dad had the ability to make instant friends in any language, and he even had a smattering of Italian. In no time at all, they were our landsmen, our friends and brothers. Their spokesman was a tough but vaguely graceful man with a keen sense of humor and, apparently, a love of children. There were women in the house, women who did the cooking and the washing and I'm not sure what else for the men, but there were no children. I wasn't sure why. The Italian capo — I guess now that was his official position, although I didn't know all that in those pre-Brando days — promised to help me with my baseball career, which I told him had languished since the time I had mistakenly tried to steal first base.

On the way home, my father explained that these men were all *mamzers*, gangsters, bootleggers — and dangerous — and I should stay away from them. I didn't believe him, of course. The alcohol, generously added to the homemade wine, produced a potent blend that resulted in a schnapps that lifted Zaideh's beard and forced him to clap a hand to the top of his yarmulke, when he sampled it later. The family switched my father's status from schlemiel to Messiah. But he wasn't satisfied. No, Dad was determined to do more than rival Rothschild; he would *better* him. In fact, he would be the first of our family to make his own champagne. Someone had told him that if he bottled the now-potent wine, and added raisins before corking the bottles tightly, the fermentation of the raisins would create a bubbly champagne unmatched in the civilized world. So Dad tried it. We must have put down about thirty quart bottles, richly raisined and tightly corked.

A few nights later, I was awakened by the sound of explosions. BANG! BANG! BANG! We all rushed down to the cellar, where the ceiling and the walls dripped with alcoholic vinegar and the concrete floor was littered with shattered glass. While my mother hollered at my father and we started to clean it up, we heard BANG! BANG! BANG! again. But there weren't any bottles left in the cellar. BANG! BANG! BANG!

We learned later that war had broken out. The New Jersey police had crossed the border in force to collect a missed payment of protection money. They were searching for the capo, who had disappeared.

Two Italian men brought him over to our house at midnight, my friend who had been teaching me baseball, his hip shattered by a bullet, blood dripping from a wound in his cheek, and they asked my parents if they would hide him until the heat was off.

My mother shouted, "No!" But for once, my father was the man of the house. I remember that the Italian was hidden in the second house in our row, and a doctor arrived who asked no questions. Our neighbor was patched up but unable to walk. We hid him for weeks.

After all, Dad said, how can you refuse a friend who let you borrow a gallon of his best alcohol to celebrate the holy Passover? And that's how my father invented champagne. The best in the civilized world.

PART IV:

MY DEFINING MOMENT; OR, DISCOVERING THE ESSENCE OF BEING JEWISH

There comes a moment — in Catholicism it's called an epiphany — when it suddenly hits you: An understanding comes to you, the spirit enters you, and you *know*. If you're Jewish, what you suddenly know is who you are, why you are a Jew. Each Jew may experience this moment, this under- standing of the essence of being Jewish, at a different time and in a different way. Or the sense of understanding may come not as the result of any single event but just slowly accumulates in the bones, in the gut, in the soul, as the experiences of daily life sink in. Once you've got it, you've got it, though, and you find you're at ease with yourself and your place in the universe. Life may still be full of mystery and, at times, sorrow, but through everything you are anchored and comforted by your own unshakable sense of

who you are at your core — you are a Jew.
That is what these stories express, each in
its own way.

— Alan King

Jerry Stiller

Jerry Stiller is an Emmy Award–nominated comedian and actor. Among his many film and television roles, he played Frank Costanza on *Seinfeld*. He is the father of Ben and Amy Stiller and husband of actress-comedian Anne Meara, who was also his comedy partner.

For reasons that go back centuries, Jews were never homogenized. We were always apart and distant from the cultures we were born in. I knew this from my mother, who arrived from Poland, from a shtetl named Frampol made famous in many of Isaac Bashevis Singer's stories. The entire Citron family arrived piecemeal, all living in the same tenement, 61 Columbia Street on the Lower East Side. My father's family, on the other hand, arrived from Austria.

When I met Isaac Bashevis Singer at an event and told him that my mother's family was from Frampol and arrived in America and lived at 61 Columbia Street, he replied, "Well, Frampol was a small town."

My mother and father met in a dairy restaurant on Rivington Street, owned by one of her older brothers. They were married, had four children, and fought like cats and dogs. Blame it on the Depression and what being a taxicab driver when few could afford to take a taxi could do to a family who couldn't put food on the table or pay rent.

My father, however, was a man who loved life. He scraped enough pennies together to take me to the Follies Theatre in Williamsburg, where we would watch five acts of vaudeville and a double feature. Remarkably, the audiences could still laugh at the live comics during those desperate days.

At night he'd turn on the Atwater Kent radio and we'd listen to Eddie Cantor, Jack Benny, Burns and Allen. I'd sit with him and the family and laugh. "They're all Jewish," my father would often say. "The Marx brothers are Jewish."

The radio and vaudeville were able to turn sadness into mirth if only for a few minutes. It was about hope. Those comedians gave us hope. In my mind I thought of the comedians as rich. How else could they joke so well if they weren't well off?

So the dream caught fire in my child's mind. If I could do this kind of work, I could pull my parents out of their misery, make them rich and make the world a better place.

One problem: I had no talent. I was a child, but a child could dream. I had a talent for dreaming. I wanted to be a Jew like Eddie Cantor, who could make you laugh and let you know he was a Jew. That was the kicker. So I worked at it. I studied, performed, and kept at it.

I married Anne on September 14, 1953, at City Hall. Anne converted to Judaism. We have two children, Amy and Ben. Both are actors. We consider being alive and working still as God's will. We attend services on High Holidays. On Passover, we have a seder or go to one and eat matzos. We have a mezuzah on our door. Yes, we're Jewish, perhaps not the kind my uncles, aunts, and parents envisioned, but still connected to the God of Abraham.

Four Things

Jamie Lee Curtis

Jamie Lee Curtis has starred in dozens of movies, including the *Halloween* series of horror films, *A Fish Called*

Wanda, My Girl, True Lies, and *Freaky Friday,* for which she received an Academy Award nomination. She is also a best-selling children's book author.

I didn't grow up Jewish. I knew that my father, Tony Curtis, was Jewish and that I have a Hebrew name, but that was about it. I went to bar mitzvahs — the party, never the services. I was married without a religion, and I am raising my daughter and son without one.

Four things finally started me connecting to my Jewish heritage. The first was the famous photograph of the young boy, hands held high, obviously terrified, from the Holocaust. I don't know more about the photograph, but I saw it and cut it out and started carrying it with me. It started connecting me to that horrific time and my ancestors and my history. His sweet, frightened face was the portal by which I entered into that grim reality.

The second thing was when my father married a Jewish woman, his fourth wife and the first Jew. He married her under his family's chuppah, and it was held high by my brothers. It was important to my father, and that made me realize how much of his

"Jewishness" he had put away during his tenure as a movie star. It made me happy to see him stand there and accept his heritage surrounded by his children. That marriage didn't last, but I believe his Jewish connection did.

The third was when my father was asked to help a group of Hungarian Jews raise money to restore and rebuild the Dohány Street Synagogue in Budapest. My father's only request was that they name the organization after his father, Emanuel Schwartz. The work of the Emanuel Foundation and the restoration of the synagogue is a beautiful tribute to the Hungarian Jews lost in the Holocaust. I am proud of my father and mostly of my sister, Kelly, who worked so hard with the Emanuel Foundation to see that goal completed.

But the strongest link for me to my Jewish heritage is through my dear friend Deborah Oppenheimer and her Oscar-winning documentary, *Into the Arms of Strangers: Stories of the Kindertransport*. As her friend, I participated like a fly on the wall through the entire enterprise: the research, the labyrinth of finding and connecting with the wonderful Kindertransport survivors, the filming, editing, presentations, accolades, and the continued bearing witness to reconnected lives and stories. This was her gift to her mother, who was a Kindertransport survivor.

Wendy Wasserstein writes, "In our lives, our friends are our family." This witnessing and being a part of this much bigger picture has brought me closer to understanding my own connection to my Jewish heritage and history.

I have much more to learn.

<hr/>

An Ethical Choice

Daniel Schorr

Daniel Schorr is senior news analyst at National Public Radio. His memoir, *Staying Tuned: A Life in Journalism*, recounts his career, which included working at CBS with Edward R. Murrow and at CNN with Ted Turner.

Released from the army in 1945, I decided that journalism would be my lifelong vocation. But not Jewish journalism, which I found too limiting. The hunt for the Jewish angle was frustrating. So I became a Jew in journalism. We Jews are searchers for the truth, sometimes called investigative reporting. Having grown up poor in the Bronx, I had a need to prove myself to the goyim. There! I've said it. But would a Jewish ethic ever cause me to kill a story that I had unearthed? It happened once.

My *CBS Reports* program "Poland — Country on a Tightrope" documented the political chill settling over Poland in 1959. My visit to Auschwitz was in my film — but not my encounter with a caravan of Jews we had run across in eastern Poland that was secretly making its way to Israel. The Jews came from a part of Poland that had been annexed by the Soviet Union, and there were several thousand more caught on the Soviet side who had survived the war and the Holocaust and were desperately anxious to leave. Israel had negotiated a delicate secret arrangement with the Soviet and Polish governments. The Jews would be "repatriated" to Poland with the understanding that they would almost immediately leave the country, bound for Israel. But there was one condition attached to the agreement. The arrangement must remain a secret. If any word became public, the Soviets would immediately cancel the arrangement. I held back a reel of film containing interviews with the Polish Jews. This was a profound violation of my journalistic ethic that a reporter has no right to interpose himself between information legitimately acquired and the public he serves.

When next I was in New York, I brought the reel of film containing the Jewish interviews with me and went to see Edward R. Murrow. He had strong pro-Israel sympathies himself. I produced the can of film and explained how, against all my principles, I had withheld it. All he said was, "I understand."

Heal the World and Pursue Justice

Peter Yarrow

Peter Yarrow is a musician, songwriter, and social activist. As a member of the Grammy Award–winning trio Peter, Paul and Mary, he wrote the classics *Puff, the Magic Dragon*; *Day Is Done*; *Light One Candle*; and *The Great Mandela*. Among the causes he has committed himself to are equal rights, peace, the environment, homelessness, and hospice care.

Like many New York City Jewish children

whose idealistic parents were born at the turn of the century, my childhood exposure to religion did not come through a temple or synagogue or religious practice in the home. It came through the unspoken messages of the way my mother treated others and me, and led her life. "Children learn by osmosis and imitation," she would say and send me off to make Sunday visits to the Ethical Culture Society of New York City. Ethical Culture preached, if you can call it that, that the practice of religion is best expressed by the ethics of our behavior — the way we lead our lives.

My mother, who was an English, speech, and drama teacher, was not a fan of organized religion. She embraced the notion that organized religion can lead to a kind of blindness of sorts and an inability to walk in each other's shoes. Such blindness, she maintained, can lead to cultural and religious self-absorption, prejudice, hatred, violence, and war. The truth is, recent history has shown her to be right in ways that I can only now fully comprehend. But the other truth is that in her advocacies, in important ways, she was also Jewish to the core in a cultural and ethical sense. She worshipped learning and the arts, and strove to advance justice and fairness in every way she could. Consequently, I grew up taking violin lessons, art lessons, and recorder lessons, and attending the Philharmonic series and never watching television because to her, television was banal and a waste of time.

Beyond that, and more important, though I never heard the words *tikkun olam* until I was in my thirties and given the language of such utterances by some of my favorite rabbi friends, such as Elliott Kleinman, Danny Syme, and Alex Schindler, I was taught the imperative of doing my part to try to heal the world and pursue justice.

All this came from my most nonreligious, and yet somehow most perfectly religious, nonobservant mother, Vera. Though I've now softened my early perspective about observance being categorically dangerous, if not anathema, I still basically adhere to that most profound view from my earliest years — which is how I grew up to be, truly, Jewish.

Larry King

Broadcasting veteran Larry King is the
host of *Larry King Live* on CNN and
the radio talk show *Larry King Weekend.*
His numerous awards and honors include the George Foster Peabody
Award for Excellence in Broadcasting.

Being Jewish is more than just a religious
faith (I lost that part a long time ago). It is
social, it is family and friends and education,
and maybe it is, above all, humor. I have
never known a Jewish person without a sense
of humor, including the ability to laugh at
yourself.

I grew up in the Bensonhurst section of
Brooklyn. My father passed away when I
was only nine and a half years old, and my
mother raised me and my younger brother,
Marty, all by herself. She kept a kosher
home. We lit the candles every Friday. I
was bar mitzvahed. You know, it's funny,
there are some facets that still have a
strong hold on me: I can never eat meat
and drink milk at the same time. I still love

matzos and potato pancakes and matzo ball soup.

One of the tales of my childhood was given to me by my mother's sister, Aunt Dora. "Do you know that nobody ever died eating matzo ball soup? Methuselah ate matzo ball soup for 850 years. One day he stopped and he died."

Being a Jew is like walking in the wind or swimming: you are touched at all points and conscious everywhere.

— Lionel Trilling

Hugs and Kisses

Gene Wilder

Gene Wilder has appeared in twenty-seven films in his forty-year career, including the classics *Blazing Saddles*, *Young Frankenstein*, and *Willy Wonka & the Chocolate Factory*. He is also a screenwriter and director.

I'm not at all religious, although I am certainly Jewish — which, to me, means that my parents hugged and kissed me a lot as I was growing up.

❧ ━━━━ ❧

And/Or

Edward Newman

Edward Newman, an All-Pro guard with the Miami Dolphins, played in two Super Bowls and four Pro Bowls during his career.

I was born three years after the State of Israel came into existence. The horror of the Holocaust was a fresh memory. Too often, the world imposed stereotyped expectations upon its Jews. But that was changing. In this regard, there is an interesting parallel between my life and that of Israel.

To convey this idea, let me describe a get-together for the Passover dinner at our house when I was about fourteen years old. All of the family was there. The seder performed, dinner finished, and Papa Harry exclaimed that once again the entire Arab League mounted an unsuccessful war against the very existence of Israel. We were more than pleased that Israel maintained one of the finest armed forces in the world.

Many thought that Jews were soft. Generally the world expected that Jews would find political solutions for their troubles. But they were wrong. Jews could fight. It was a new thing to identify Jews as great warriors.

Then, Nana Anna inquired, "*Tatteleh,* how is school going? Don't you want to be a doctor like your uncles Lenny and Chuck? You have to study if you want to amount to anything."

Mom voiced her opinion: "You are spending too much time with that football and wrestling."

Dad sat pensively by.

It was clear from the beginning that I was a superior athlete. Nonetheless, my folks always emphasized the academics. This has been the dilemma for Jewish athletes since ancient times. What is the worthwhile objective: Should one develop the mind or the body?

That Sunday, Dad said, "C'mon, son, let's go to the deli for bagels and lox." That was pretext. He wanted to philosophize. He explained that each person chooses a path. A good life is one where the world is a better place for that person having passed through it. Dad concluded that a "good life path" could center on the mind and/or the body.

I love that and/or option. The life of the mind and of the body are not mutually exclusive. So I studied my books. And I worked extra hard at the wrestling and football. This effort got me a scholarship to Duke University, and I graduated with a degree in psychology. By this effort, I was drafted by the Miami Dolphins, for whom I played for thirteen years. I was named All-Pro four times, and in my era the Dolphins went to three Super Bowls.

So I was playing professional football, and I was doing it quite well. I made no secret about my being Jewish. The fans, the coaches, the players — they all got something that they did not expect. They thought Jews were not tough enough to play pro ball. Well, Israeli troops prove how tough Jews can be, and in roughly the same time frame, so does Ed Newman. I love shattering stereotypes. I hope that I was a role model for many young aspiring Jewish athletes.

Toward the end of my football career, I was admitted to the University of Miami School of Law. I got my degree, passed the bar exam, and then practiced law for seven years. In 1994, the good people of Miami–Dade County, Florida, elected me judge. All this is in consequence of a "good life path" that encompassed both the mind and the body.

Thanks, Dad. You were right. I am still doing the good. I just wish I could play a better round of golf. Football is for young fellows.

> There are two ways to live your life. One is as though nothing is a miracle. The other is as though everything is a miracle.
>
> — Albert Einstein

What Keeps Us Going

Sid Caesar

Sid Caesar is an award-winning comedian and veteran of Broadway, film, and television. He is a member of the Television Hall of Fame.

The keeper of the flame: Jewish humor.

> Look at Jewish history. Unrelieved lamenting would be intolerable. So, for every ten Jews beating their breasts, God designated one to be crazy and amuse the breast-beaters. By the time I was five, I knew I was that one.
>
> — Mel Brooks

A Worried Jew

Judd Hirsch

Judd Hirsch won two Emmys for his role on the hit television series *Taxi* and two Tonys for his roles in the Broadway plays *I'm Not Rappaport* and *Conversations with My Father*. Among his movie credits, he played Jeff Goldblum's father in the blockbuster hit *Independence Day*.

Where I grew up, being Jewish meant knowing the risks of venturing by foot out of the neighborhood. There were safe routes and there were no-man's-lands. But I wasn't old enough or simply informed enough to know why — from ignorance, perhaps, but I'd like to think from innocence. Even at seder, I wondered why the spirit we invited in to drink from the extra cup of wine never made so much as a discernible dent in the amount in the cup. I imagined the tiniest invisible hummingbird with a yarmulke. And to be considered a man at thirteen was an unfathomable idea — I was so short and so unformed in certain areas that it made my head swim just to think of what I was expected to do with a thirteen-year-old girl. I could only pray that when I was bar mitzvahed I'd get my promised Voit basketball (and not the condoms, which wouldn't fit, anyhow). Growing up Jewish was so confusing that it gives truth to the saying: A worried Jew is a happy Jew.

<hr />

My Mezuzah

David Copperfield

David Copperfield is an award-winning magician who tours worldwide, stars in network television specials, and had his own Broadway show.

My mother, Rebecca, was born in Israel — she's a sabra. My dad was born in Brooklyn, which in those days was the Israel of the East Coast. His parents were Russian Jews. And the family name is not Copperfield but

Copper*feld*. (Just kidding. It's Kotkin, a Russian word that means "Son of Dickens.")

I grew up in New Jersey and went to Hebrew school and Jewish summer camps. But at home, although we knew we were Jewish, we weren't formal about it or observant. On Passover, we held a seder, but my mother made sure to dye the hard-boiled egg a festive color so Christian guests would feel at home. My parents taught me the basics of Reform Judaism: pork is forbidden, except in Chinese food. Lobster is shellfish and *traif* unless someone else is paying. It's important to marry within the faith, and equally important to gain as much experience as possible with girls outside the faith. At my bar mitzvah, I read aloud from the Torah, got through all the prayers, and did a double-dove production from my tallith. The rabbi said, "Today you are a man — and a meshuggener."

Jewishness wasn't something I thought much about. There were Jewish kids in my high school. We had an unofficial club, the UnAthletics. But basically being Jewish when I was growing up was a fact of life, like air or background music, something you're comfortable with and take for granted.

Looking back, I'm really glad I went to Hebrew school and learned as much as I did about Judaism. In fact, I wish I had learned more. An Orthodox friend, the movie producer Arthur Cohn, recently sent me a mezuzah and I didn't know whether it was supposed to go outside or inside the front door. I was too embarrassed to ask Arthur, so I called a rabbi, who said it had to go on the outside of the door unless there was a real risk it would get stolen. I'd already had it installed inside the front door. I asked the rabbi if I had to take it down and reinstall it. He said, "Nah. If anyone asks why you put it inside the doorway, just tell 'em you're a Polish Jew."

I was raised by secular Jews who had a strong Jewish identification, although they weren't religious. My parents believed in an ethical, idealistic way of life. I always assumed that that's what Jews were all about. That and storytelling — we have a tradition of great Jewish storytellers. Just look at the Bible.

— Grace Paley

Nathaniel Rosen

Nathaniel Rosen has been playing the cello since the age of six. In 1978 he won the Gold Medal at the Tchaikovsky International Competition, the only American cellist ever to do so. He has released many recordings and served as principal cellist with the Los Angeles Chamber Orchestra.

My father supported his family as a cantor while going to law school but lost his job after confessing to the rabbi that he was an atheist. I went to shul only with my grandfather, whose Torah readings were the essential art of biblical Hebrew, resonant forever. At home, we were a bacon-but-not-pork family and at Chinese restaurants we ate spareribs well cooked. Our Friday Shabbat celebrations were informal performances of string quartets of Mozart, Beethoven, Schumann, and Haydn. You can't get closer to God than that.

Barry Louis Polisar

Barry Louis Polisar, a four-time Parents' Choice Award winner, writes books and music for children. He has written songs for *Sesame Street* and *My Weekly Reader*, and his songs are also featured on The Learning Channel.

My family was not very religious. I had a "Tijuana bar mitzvah." I was given a crash course education with Hebrew lessons less than a year before my bar mitzvah. I remember thinking at the time that it was a meaningless exercise, and in a way, it was, because it had little meaning in my family's life. We knew we were Jews, but we never went to synagogue and did not celebrate the holidays.

One year I decided I would fast on Yom Kippur. I remember my grandmother trying to feed me her homemade matzo ball soup — her sense of Jewish identity. My grandmother was a free-thinker, rebelling against the orthodoxy of her own mother and, like many of her generation, happy to assimilate into the great American culture.

My grandmother told me a story that her father, Louis, used to tell about God giving the Jewish people religion. "It's really not such a hard religion," God said. "Here, I'll write it down for you. You try it for a while and if it doesn't suit you, bring it back." So the Jewish people tried it and found it was too hard. For days, caravan upon caravan stretched across the desert carrying Haftorahs, mezuzahs, yarmulkes, prayer shawls, commentaries, and prayer books. God looked out at the caravans that stretched to the horizon and said, "What's all this? All I wrote down for you were ten simple commandments."

Of course, I later realized there is more to Judaism than ten commandments. The full story is actually many, many stories — rich with history, irony, and lessons for our own lives.

And stories shape our lives.

When I was in college I began taking classes in Jewish literature. I read the Yiddish poets and short story writers and read the later American Jewish writers. They all had one thing in common: They were writing secular works and were rebelling against the strict orthodoxies of their religion, but the values of their religion kept creeping into everything they wrote.

Then I found the Hasidic story that really had resonance for me: Years ago, a rabbi in Eastern Europe saw that his village was about to be destroyed in a pogrom. He went to a certain part of the forest, lit a fire, and said a special prayer, and his village was spared. A generation later, another threat was upon the village and another rabbi went to the same place in the forest and lit a fire, but he did not know the prayer. Still later, another rabbi, in order to save his people once more, went into the forest. He did not know the prayer or even how to light the fire. Finally, there was another threat and another rabbi. He was unable to light the fire, did not know the prayer, and couldn't even find the place in the forest.

As I read that story, I realized that with each passing generation, my *own* family had lost more and more of what had gone before and I was about to be the last link of that chain. I realized that without a deliberate effort, my Jewish heritage would be so diminished that soon, no one in my family would be able to say the prayers, light the fire, or find *our* place in the forest.

Years later, I promised my kids — twins — that when they went to synagogue for services, I would never just drop them off but would join them in the sanctuary. At their b'nai mitzvah on Rosh Khodesh, I watched them read Hebrew and chant from the Torah.

Rosh Khodesh celebrates a new month in the Jewish calendar and is a reminder to us all that life is fleeting. We are taught to use each precious moment wisely so that no day will pass without bringing us closer to some worthy achievement. I reminded my children that a mitzvah is a command-ment, but the work also means a good work, an ethical deed. As my children en-tered into adulthood, I hoped they would do well and asked each of them also to do good.

A Jew by Politics and Art

Nicholas Meyer

Nicholas Meyer wrote the best-selling book and the Academy Award–nomi-nated screenplay *The Seven-Per-Cent Solution*. He also directed *Star Trek II: The Wrath of Kahn* and *Star Trek VI: The Undiscovered Country*.

I grew up in Manhattan after the war, the

privileged child of middle-class parents. My American-born father was a psychoanalyst (what Hitler scoffed at as the Jewish science), and my Russian-born mother was a concert pianist. Though my parents were both Jewish, neither had any religious upbringing and passed none on to me. My father was not bar mitzvahed and, unsurprisingly, neither was I. I don't believe that my grandfathers were, either. Art and various leftist political philosophies constituted the family religion. My father was conversant with the Old and New Testaments as literature and referred to them in his work. In later years, he made no secret of his regret for his ignorance, particularly the fact that he didn't speak Yiddish, but his regrets were intellectual and emotional, never religious in origin or emphasis.

Growing up in a cultural hothouse, I thought Jews were people who read books with hard covers, performed chamber music in their living rooms, and thought Adlai Stevenson was the cat's pajamas.

In this state of (blissful?) ignorance, I played with my neighborhood friend, Johnny Benedict, a Catholic boy my age whose parents ran the candy store on the corner. Johnny had the benefit of a religious education that conferred upon him an enormous intellectual advantage. He patiently explained that my family and I were damned because we did not accept Jesus as our savior. I was heard to reply, "Well, we're Jewish and we believe in wolves."

No one, including me, was able to explain satisfactorily what this meant. What it revealed was clear enough. My parents found my ignorance a source of amusement, but to me, faced with daily theological debates with my friend, it was a real problem. I therefore asked my parents to send me to Sunday school so I could learn. I was duly dispatched to the Sunday school of Temple Emanu-El on Fifth Avenue, where I stayed for some weeks before being expelled. Apparently, in response to some piece of indoctrination, I responded, "I don't believe that and, what's more, I don't think you do, either." This concluded my formal religious training. Everything else I learned about being Jewish was gleaned from Hollywood epics such as *The Ten Commandments* (which I loved), *Solomon and Sheba*, and subsequently John Huston's *The Bible*.

My sense of personal identity is profoundly connected to my perception of myself as a Jew, but I remain at a loss to understand precisely what this means. With no religious background, training, or inclination, my Jewishness remains largely cultural. I am a liberal Democrat; my religion, like my parents', is art.

> I find television very educating. Every time somebody turns on the set, I go into the other room and read a book.
> — Groucho Marx

A Jew by Chance

David Margolis

David Margolis is a contributing editor of *The Jerusalem Report*. He is also the author of two novels, *Change of Partners* and *The Stepman*; a volume of short fiction, *The Time of Wandering*; as well as coauthor (with David Matzner) of *The Muselmann*, a Holocaust memoir.

We kept kosher — "because we're Jewish," which was as close to ideology as we came. But we made compromises, such as going out for Chinese food on Sunday afternoons. On one such excursion when I was ten years old, my older brother announced at table something he'd learned recently: Spareribs are from a pig, not, as my mother claimed to believe, from a cow. Spareribs are *pork!*

As I sat there, a wondrously greasy rib in my paw, my parents discussed whether I should be permitted to raise the rib to my mouth. They riffled through some private Talmud containing special extra-halachic categories until my mother, the religious judge in our household, handed down her ruling: "Since he's been eating them all along, it's okay." Saved on Sunday, I gnawed the saucy spareribs to the bone.

Around the same time — this was in the mid-1950s, that dreary decade — the question arose both at our family table and in my Sunday school class: If the United States and Israel were at war, which side should American Jews be on? The approved answer in both councils — I remember saying these words to win my Sunday school teacher's approval — was, "We're Americans first and Jews second."

This was not an instruction (as it should have been) in subtext, in what it served us as Americans to tell the goyim, but an expression of what an entire community of Jews accepted as revealed truth. Being Jewish was a secondary identity.

For my bar mitzvah, they stuffed me into an itchy suit, surrounded me with strangers, arranged for me to learn a Haftorah in transliteration, that Hebrew antipoetry of meaningless sounds, and produced the required glitzy "affair." I understood nothing of what I did or, worse, why I did it, and — worst of all — nobody saw anything wrong with that. The lesson was: Subordinate meaning and feeling to appearance. Today you are a man.

Having learned that Judaism is false pretenses, I fled from it as soon and as far as I could. All that remained was an inchoate inner knowledge that I was "Jewish." I didn't deny it, but neither was I very interested in it.

Only coincidence and luck brought me back. I married a Jew, and once I had children to raise and saw them becoming secularized Americans whose grandparents had been Jewish, something primal inside me rejected that. Coincidentally (if you believe in coincidence), about the same time, a research and writing project opened up for me the wildness, subtlety, and complexity of Jewish learning and history, something no one had ever shown me. Pursuing it, I found teachers and community and remade my life. I sometimes call myself a "Jew by chance."

Very many American Jewish children are still raised, as I was, without consistency, commitment, or community, without Jewish knowledge, love for the Jewish past, or special solidarity with other Jews, and with a shocking ambivalence toward that near-miraculous culmination of Jewish history, the world's only self-governing Jewish state.

As I look back, I see my Jewish upbringing as an inheritance of confusion that expressed a failure of Jewish communal nerve. The American Jewish community certainly has a lot of strengths. God willing, we will find new ways to raise our children as proud, committed, and creative Jews.

Lessons from the Yiddish Shule

Arthur Hiller

Arthur Hiller is the director of more than thirty movies, including *Love Story; Man of La Mancha; See No Evil, Hear No Evil;* and *Outrageous Fortune.*

My parents loved culture and they loved

their Jewish heritage. Indeed, in 1930 they started a Yiddish theater in Edmonton, Alberta, where they had immigrated to (from Poland, via New York) in 1912. They weren't professionals in theater, they just wanted to do a Yiddish play once or twice a year for the Jewish community of 450 to keep in touch with their heritage.

So when I was seven or eight years old, I was helping the man building and decorating the sets. By the time I was eleven, I was acting with the long beard and the payess. Little did I know that the love of theater and music and literature they instilled in me would one day lead to a career directing films. And I shouldn't forget that Papa bought me a camera when I was six years old because I wanted to take pictures like he always did.

I remember my father's wish always being that he would see my name on the flyleaf of a book. Needless to say, he was happy seeing my credit on a television show.

I'm also so happy that my dear parents, with a group of friends, started a Yiddish *shule*, where I learned Yiddish and read Sholem Aleichem, I. L. Peretz, and all the "workers' writers," as I called them. As they always said: *"Besser a mensch und nischt a Yid, vi a Yid und nischt a mensch"* (better a good person and not a Jew, than a Jew and not a good person). All this strengthened the moral values my parents instilled in me by their own way of living and by their teachings. Also, once or twice a year, the *shule* group would bring out a speaker or writer or singer of Jewish stories or song. I even remember sharing my bedroom with the composer of "My Yiddishe Mama."

Speaking Yiddish also came in handy when my wife and I first started traveling to Europe in the late fifties. At that time French was the international language, and outside of the British Commonwealth few people spoke English. Somehow we could always find someone who spoke Yiddish who could direct us where we wanted to go or help us with our problems.

Tikkun Olam

Judy Chicago

Judy Chicago is an artist and author whose works include *The Dinner Party*, a multimedia project that symbolizes the history of women in Western civilization.

I always knew I was Jewish despite the fact that my parents — left-wing intellectuals with an avid interest in history and social change with an equally avid distaste for all things Jewish — were not at all observant. Nevertheless, my father, who was descended from twenty-three unbroken generations of rabbis until he rejected the tradition in favor of union organizing ("not to worry, my dear," one rabbi told me later, "Moses was the first union organizer"), repeatedly told me that I had "blue blood." The reason for this seemingly illustrious condition was that I am directly descended on both my paternal and maternal grandparents' sides from the great seventeenth-century rabbi and teacher, the Vilna Gaon.

Despite never darkening the door of any temple until my late teens and knowing next to nothing about what it meant to be Jewish (not to mention that — even though I was born in 1939 — the Holocaust was never mentioned, which is why I took up an aesthetic inquiry about it many years later), I was raised in the tradition of Jewish values, i.e., with a commitment to social justice. And without ever knowing the term, I realized later in life that I must have imbibed the concept of *tikkun olam* (the healing or repairing of the world) through my mother's milk. For it shaped my life and work — so, in retrospect, it seems clear that the traditions of both Jewish and feminist thought have come together to make Judy (Cohen) Chicago who she is today.

We must once again be dreamers of a better world, binding our children to us with the intensity of our moral worth, the beauty of our historical and ethical vision. Our children will join us if they see us engaged in the heroic and moral journey of Jewish identity — at least they should.

— Anne Roiphe

Food and Laughter

Bernie Brillstein

Bernie Brillstein is the founding partner of Brillstein Grey Entertainment and has served as executive producer of many television shows and movies, including *Just Shoot Me*, *NewsRadio*, *Happy Gilmore*, *Dragnet*, and *The Blues Brothers*.

My father was a Conservative Jew and the president of his little synagogue in the millinery district in New York City. Still, I'd call myself more of a traditional Jew than a religious one. I sincerely believe God is up there watching us, keeping the big book on how we act in life, but I've never lived in a kosher home, and I never much liked to go to temple. In fact, I did my bar mitzvah phonetically. *Ba-ruch A-tah.* The rabbi even had to teach me how to make the "chh" sound. Fortunately, this sound is easy for Jews, I guess from going to "eech" and "uchh" and "acch" all the time. To us, "chh" is not a sound, it's a word.

However, on the High Holidays my father would insist that I go to temple, so I'd sit there while the rabbi and the cantor carried on, staring at the old men davening. For some reason that made me feel warm and good inside, even though I wondered if I even believed in Moses.

Every so often I'd turn around and look to the back of the synagogue and see my father standing there, wearing a yarmulke and a tallith, and holding a prayer book. But instead of being lost in deep meditation, he'd be looking at the rabbi and then at his watch. I knew that about a quarter to six he'd raise his finger and move it in a circle, trying to catch the rabbi's eye. This wasn't some ecstatic expression of religious fervor. My father was telling him, "Wrap it up." Why? The sun was going down, it was almost time to eat, and he was hungry. Wrap it up. Let's get out of here. My father did this every year. I thought it was hilarious.

My father wanted his dinner, and those dinners — after the Yom Kippur fast, or during the Passover seder — are my fondest memory of growing up Jewish. We always had lots of food and booze, though as Jews we cared much more about the food than the liquor. You go to a white-bread affair and there's a lot of liquor and the food is terrible. Don't ask me why.

When I tell you it was all about the food, I mean it. My father's Passover ritual usually took a minute and a half. We didn't even read from the Haggadahs. No one hid the afikomen. I didn't ask one question, let alone four.

The guests were usually the same, and God forbid if you didn't attend, because you'd hear, "What? Are you too big now?" There was my father's brother Lou and his wife, Lilly. They lived on Long Island. Invariably, my father would say, "So, you think you're big shots?" The loving sarcasm and disdain were unmistakable. Also at dinner was my father's sister Eva and her husband, Max. They lived in the Bronx, and Max had made some good money during the war. Also big shots. And my uncle Jack — the real big shot — a well-known comedian, and his wife, Winnie, a Ziegfeld girl. My brother, Sam; my mother, Tillie; my father, Moe; and I rounded out the group.

If the guests were the same, so was the food. Gefilte fish, matzo ball soup with plenty of chicken fat floating on the surface, kugel, pot roast, pies for dessert. I've never forgotten the smells combining in the air, settling on our clothes, and the compliments my mother — who cooked only once or twice a year — would get: "Such soft matzo balls, Tillie," or "That's the best gefilte fish you've ever made."

My father would sit at the head of the table, drinking scotch and stabbing at pieces of challah with his fork.

And the fights: every year, also the same. My father and uncles always battled over issues important and insignificant. They'd scream and yell — and end up laughing — while I got diarrhea until I got old enough to understand that the whole routine was a cleansing ritual. A lot of tsuris and a lot of humor, and never a grudge afterward.

Jews are lucky that way. When gentiles fight at dinner they end up not talking to each other ever again, and then their children don't talk, either. And years later no one remembers why. Jews have a natural and irreverent sense of humor. With all the years of suffering, we had to do something just to cope. That's why a fight is just a fight — one minute screaming, the next laughing — and not something you end up sorting out in probate.

I remember one argument was about the mobster Frank Costello. He was behind the Copacabana club, and my uncle Jack, being an entertainer, knew him. My father said, "That killer. Don't you ever introduce my son to that killer."

Uncle Jack said, "I already have. At the Stork Club."

My father stared and said, "How dare you do that!"

Then the screaming started and faces turned the color of borscht. My mother let it go on for a few minutes, and then, maybe because she was nervous, or had just had enough, she put up her finger and moved it in a circle. Wrap it up. Time to calm down. Then it was back to the food, and more red faces, but this time from laughter.

* * *

Listen

Alan Shapiro

Alan Shapiro's eighth book of poems, *Song & Dance*, is an elegy for his brother, David, who died of cancer. His fifth book, *Mixed Company*, won a *Los Angeles Times* book award.

I'm facing my mother in the cramped living room of her small apartment in Chapel Hill, North Carolina. She and my father have recently moved here from California. She's seventy-nine, he's eighty-five. He with his Parkinson's and macular degeneration, she with terrible arthritis in her back and hands — they have started over in a new place where aside from me and my wife and kids they do not know a soul. As my mother explains it to her few remaining friends and family, they didn't want me having to traipse across the continent to care for them every time something happened. Better for me to have them living here.

She's struggled up out of her recliner, panting from the effort, and has handed me the list of groceries I should get, if it's not too much trouble.

"Wait," she says, as I turn to go. "Wait. Use my car. Let it be on my nickel."

I tell her no, I'd rather use my own. Her radio's on the blink.

"Take the keys," she says. "Take. How far do you have to go that you have to listen?"

The question pulls me up short, disorients me, thrills and annoys me all at once. It's not just the tinge of Yiddish in the syntax but also the stubbornness masquerading as request, the double exposure in the tone of generosity and distrust, of pride and need, that suddenly conjures out of thin air the kitchen table in the old house in Brookline, Massachusetts, where the elders sat and kibitzed. I could be ten years old again, or five, or even younger, too young to count as company, absorbing without quite knowing that I am the second-hand smoke of their inflections and intonations.

I say it over to myself: How far do you have to go that you have to listen? I hum it; I chant it like a mantra, as if it were itself the music of my childhood, the verbal key to an immigrant culture that's nearly now extinct, that goes on living in my mother's and father's voices, if nowhere else. I think of how my parents got here, of everything they had to suffer: not just the painful but inevitable losses that come with having lived a long, full life — the death of parents, relatives, nearly all of the friends who once had sat around that kitchen table — but the unnatural devastations too — the breast cancer that killed their daughter in 1995, the brain cancer that killed their son a few years later. I think of the unthinkable — what it would be like to bury one of my own children, and I'm amazed my parents have gotten here at all. What could possibly have held their lives together in the face of so much shattering?

My mother stares me down, her one remaining child, and says again, in case I didn't hear the first time, "So? How far do you have to go that you have to listen?"

Not far at all, I want to tell her. But I know it's not an answer that she wants. She wants I should only take the keys. So I do.

> I really care about what happens to
> people. I came from a very solid Mid-
> western Jewish home . . . I led a very
> sheltered life. I had never seen a man
> hit his wife. I had never seen any
> drunkenness. I had never seen any pov-
> erty. I knew these things were hap-
> pening, but they never happened to me.
> The mail grew me up in a hurry.
> — Esther Lederer (Ann Landers)

The Tree in the Log

Dina Rosenfeld

Dina Rosenfeld is editor in chief of
Hachai Publishing and the author of
many Jewish children's books, including
*The Very Best Place for a Penny, A Tree
Full of Mitzvos,* and *A Chanukah Story
for Night Number Three.*

So, there we were in 1968 at Zylphia Ford's
sixth birthday party. She had to travel by bus
every day to our white Jewish neighborhood
for school; the least our parents felt they
could do was carpool us to her party.

We'd been warned to be polite, to say
"thank you" to her parents, to be on our

best behavior, like junior ambassadors representing both our race and our religion on our first social visit to a black family.

More than thirty years later, I remember my fascination with the December decorations in that house. It was just like on television! Holiday cards lined the mantel, evergreen branches dotted with little lights covered the banister, and a star winked down at us from the top of a fully decorated tree.

Everything went along swimmingly, from pin the tail on the donkey to musical chairs, and at last, it was time for the cake. This wasn't like any cake we'd ever seen. This was an exotic treat, an ice cream log that Zylphia's dad cut into portions and dished out onto paper plates.

And there, in the center of each slice, was a green holiday tree! All the kids were delighted. How did they get that tree shape into the middle of the ice cream? They sang "Happy Birthday" and dug in with enthusiasm.

I couldn't believe it! In my six-year-old mind, eating a Christmas tree was like converting! How could all my Jewish friends do this? Should I leave the ice cream untouched? No, insulting my hosts that way was truly unthinkable. Not to mention that

I really, really liked ice cream.

Slowly, I started nibbling around the edges of the creamy vanilla slice. I inched closer and closer to the center but never tasted even a molecule of the forbidden tree. Like the courageous Jewish heroes of old, I wouldn't betray my faith!

Shortly after that, my family and I began to keep kosher and observe Shabbat. And happily, today I am raising children of my own committed to Judaism and a Torah lifestyle.

Yet it was abundantly clear to me all those years ago, that like a green tree in the middle of an ice cream log, my Jewish identity was at the very core of who I was — and who I would become.

<hr />

A Passion for Being Jewish

Susannah Heschel

Susannah Heschel is Eli Black Associate Professor of Jewish Studies at Dartmouth College.

All of us struggle with the problem of how to transmit our commitment to Judaism to the next generation. There are all sorts of suggestions but no solutions. How do we reproduce ourselves Jewishly?

I have a passion for Jewishness, for every manifestation of it, from Workmen's Circle to Hasidic *shtiebls*. My passion came to me as mother's milk, from wanting to emulate the Jews around me.

My father, Rabbi Abraham Joshua Heschel, used to say, "I have a daughter. I love her dearly. And I would like her to obey the commandments of the Torah. I would like her to revere me as her father. And I ask myself the question again and again, What is there about me that would be worthy of her reverence? Unless I live a life that would deserve her reverence, I would make it impossible for her to live a life of Judaism."

For both of my parents, childhood was not easy. My mother grew up during the Depression, and at the same time her father lost his eyesight due to diabetes. My father's father died when he was nine, and he and his mother and siblings were left in terrible poverty in Warsaw. Yet while my father was deprived of a father, he spoke of being surrounded by Jews who inspired his reverence and emulation. He often said that his greatest gift was to grow up around people of spiritual nobility. He writes, "In my childhood and in my youth

I was the recipient of many blessings. I lived in the presence of quite a number of extraordinary persons I could revere. And just as I lived as a child in their presence, their presence continues to live in me as an adult."

I've often wondered how to explain the phrase "religious nobility." What kind of person is worthy of that description? What inner sensibilities and values have to be cultivated to produce such a person? Like my father, I feel I was privileged to have been exposed to people of religious nobility: my father, my uncle, and a few other people, some of whom I met only briefly. Each left me with a sense of awe that a human being is capable of such extraordinary spiritual refinement.

Jewish texts tell us that human beings are made in the image of God and that it is our duty to imitate God in our lives. What is it to be created in the image of God? To be a reminder of God, my father wrote. You should look at someone and think of God. And that, in turn, means that our imperative is to live our lives in such a way that if someone looks at us, he or she is reminded of God. Such are the people of spiritual nobility who surrounded my father.

Such was his life, too. The opposite of

good is not evil, he wrote; the opposite of good is indifference. When he looked at human beings, even the most dissolute, he saw the divine image. For him, it was impossible to be indifferent to the suffering in our society caused by social inequality and the civilian tragedies incurred by war. I saw him in pain, sleepless and agonizing over the miseries of human beings.

Simply to teach that human beings are made in the image of God is not a solution to the rising rates of intermarriage and assimilation. I don't think there are any easy answers. But I do believe that both of my parents taught me how I must transmit my Jewishness to my children: to lead a life worthy of their reverence and emulation. I want to expose them to people of religious nobility, of spiritual refinement and delicacy. I want them to learn that the greatest gift is compassion, and that callousness and indifference are antithetical to the life of a Jew, who has commitments to society as well as family. Because I grew up in the presence of people who inspired me with awe, their presence continues in me, and one day, I hope, will become part of my children's lives as well.

"What Are We?"

Anne Bernays

Anne Bernays has written eight novels
and cowritten three nonfiction books,
including *Back Then: Two Literary Lives
in 1950s New York* and *The Language of
Names*.

Growing Up Jewish. I didn't. That is, both
my parents were Jewish, but it should be understood that we're talking about two
assimilationist German Jews in New York
City in the 1930s. My father was determined
to be seen as more American than as any
other denomination. When I was around six
years old, it occurred to me that the tree of
which I was a tiny branch was as exotic to
most of my Brearley School classmates as a
plate of kugel would have been to Princess
Margaret Rose — and not in a particularly
good way, either. I asked my father what we
were.

He asked what I meant by this.

"What religion are we?"

"We're nothing," he said. "But if you want to be something, you can choose your religion when you're grown up."

I knew my father's answer was specious but only in the deepest sense. He was nothing because he didn't believe in God and had no respect for religion in any form or shape.

Given this sort of religious "education," it's easy to see why I grew up baffled and vulnerable. Jews were other people, not me. It wasn't until I had my own children that I understood what being Jewish was all about. As for God: Either he's a sadist or he doesn't exist. I prefer to believe the latter. But I love tradition, ritual, and the qualities that go into making a true Jew — along with our obsession with analytic thought and our irony and self-mocking humor.

Admittedly, part of my relatively new-found pleasure in being Jewish comes from the fact that nowadays not only is anti-Semitism — at least in the United States — not nearly so threatening as it was once, but it seems as if everybody, including a presidential candidate, wants to claim at least a few drops of Jewish blood. Being

Jewish might even be considered cool. Who would have guessed?

My husband and I light candles on Friday night. Next October we're going to the bar mitzvah of our fourth grandchild, as we did to his older brother's. My father is spinning like crazy in his grave.

Every Gesture, Every Decision I Make

Uri Geller

Uri Geller is a paranormalist and the author of fifteen best-selling books.

People have always asked me what it was like to grow up psychic. But now I'm being asked what it was like to grow up Jewish.

Alan King and I first bumped into each other around 1970, in Jaffa. He was a master of his audience even then, a walking encyclopedia of gags with lightning reflexes and a memory like a computer.

I watched his faultless, instinctive timing as he tried out punch lines on friends and got laughs from people who must have heard the jokes twenty or thirty times already. He was a perfectionist and a completist, and I was not even slightly surprised when his *Great Jewish Joke Book* gathered together just about every rib-tickler worth remembering.

(This is my favorite Alan King joke: Mrs. Cohen is yelling at the lifeguard who has just pulled her husband out of the ocean. He tells her he is going to give artificial respiration. She yells back, "You'll either give my Benny real respiration or nothing!")

So I was delighted to get Alan's request to recount stories of what it was like to grow up Jewish. My first reaction was to send Alan a potted version of my autobiography, from my earliest memories of my cot in Tel Aviv to my service in the Israeli forces as a paratrooper. But when I read the letter again, I realized he wasn't interested in life stories: He wanted the essence. The defining memories.

And for me, "growing up Jewish" wasn't the essence of my childhood. It wasn't even "growing up psychic." What defined my existence was "growing up Israeli."

My mother had fled the Nazis, my father had fought to throw the British out of Palestine, and I was a boy in fifties Israel when we expected an attack any day that would, as the hostile Arab states that surrounded us swore to do, "drive the Jews into the sea."

Israel was on the defensive every day of my childhood, and this state of near paranoia climaxed when I reached my twenties, with the Six-Day War. I lived in a country that wasn't recognized by much of the world, that was peopled with survivors of Hitler's systematic attempt to wipe Jews from the face of an Aryan Earth, and that defined itself as a religious state at a time when most nations were taking God out of politics.

I have not lived in Israel for many years. My family settled in Britain in the eighties for the sake of my career, and my children can't remember living anywhere else.

I haven't lived in Israel, but Israel lives in me. I don't even have to think consciously about my homeland: I express my national culture in every gesture I make and every decision I take.

And in every word I speak — as impressionists love to remind me, my Israeli accent has never softened in thirty years of using English daily. Perhaps that's because Hanna, my wife, also an Israeli, and I use Hebrew around the home.

I was rarely conscious of being Jewish until my parents split up. Till then, when I was about ten years old, my family's faith was as unremarkable as the apartment we shared and the food we ate. Of course we were Jewish — we also sat on chairs, put shoes on our feet, and used cutlery when we ate. Anything else would have been odd.

As a matter of fact, odd things did happen to our family cutlery . . . but I believe that would have happened even if I'd been born Muslim or Confucian.

I truly became aware that I was Jewish, and that this was something to be proud of, when I was sent to stay with the Shomrons, a Hungarian-born family who lived in Kibbutz Hatzor. This communal farm near Ashdod, a long way south of the home and the mother I was leaving, strove to take children from broken homes and give them a stable upbringing.

I didn't want a stable upbringing — I wanted my Aba and Muti, my parents. And I wanted my dog, Joker.

We could faintly hear the fighting during the Suez War, and I will always cherish the memory of my father racing up to the kibbutz in his battle Jeep, caked in dust, a rifle over his shoulder. He had taken a few hours' leave from the front to visit me, and I was so proud of him.

The people of Kibbutz Hatzor were the most observant Jews I ever lived among. Within two years, I was living in Cyprus with my mother and her new husband, and my school was a Christian one — they don't have many kibbutzes in Cyprus.

I was even given a Christian name, George, which the priests claimed was the equivalent of Uri. It's still one of the few things I can't bear, to be addressed as George by friends who knew me from those days.

My Jewish faith has become deeper as I've gained in years and experience, and my awareness that I am Jewish is far more intense. So perhaps the most truthful response I can make in answer to this question is: I am still growing up Jewish.

REMEMBERING
ALAN KING

After Alan King's death on May 9, 2004, Rick Moranis, Barbara Walters, and Billy Crystal sent in their memories of working with Alan, in place of a childhood memory of growing up Jewish. Billy Crystal and Barbara Walters also delivered their remembrances of Alan King as eulogies at his funeral service on May 11, 2004.

Rick Moranis

Rick Moranis, first famous as part of the Second City comedy team, has starred in many movies, including *Spaceballs*; *Little Shop of Horrors*; *Honey, I Shrunk the Kids* and sequels; *Ghostbusters*; *Parenthood*; *My Blue Heaven*; *L.A. Story*; and *The Flintstones*.

In 1985, my friend Joel Silver, the Hollywood producer, and I concocted an idea for a movie, the sole purpose of which was to try to get Universal Studios to fly us to Las Vegas so we could meet and hang out for a couple of days with one of our comedy idols, Don Rickles. We pulled it off: got to Vegas and had an absolutely hilarious time.

Then I wound up having to write the movie.

So I enlisted the help of two writers from the Second City comedy TV show, Dick Blasucci and Paul Flaherty, and the three of us set up shop near Joel's office, ordered a slew of office supplies, a coffeemaker, and a fridge stocked full of Cokes and Heinekens, and hammered out what we thought was a pretty good script.

The idea was loosely based on Joel's experiences producing movies with Burt Reynolds. It told the story of a funny and decent actor, who, having gotten typecast as an action hero, reluctantly kept making the lucrative pictures he was growing to disdain. We called it *Killer Charlie V* and it revolved around the release of *Killer Charlie IV* and the actor's vain resistance to commit to yet another sequel.

Rickles, whom we all loved, wasn't quite right for the part after all and, though the studio was pushing to rework the movie for very hot Rodney Dangerfield, there was one and only one actor we wanted in the role: Alan King.

Like most guys my age, I'd grown up watching Alan King perform his stand-up monologues on *The Ed Sullivan Show*. I loved his confidence, his voice, and the way he dressed up in those dark tailored three-piece suits, waving his cigar like a baton, playing those audiences like a maestro of flawless rhythms and perfect pitch. In some strange way, even back then, I felt like I should know him. Was he an uncle I somehow hadn't yet met? Or a future boss I'd better not disappoint? Or perhaps, just maybe, if I could finally work up the nerve to ask Susan Kleinerman for a date, would he be her father?

We sent Alan the script. A few days later Joel got the call. Alan King wanted to meet.

I did my best to look smart that day. If I'd had a three-piece suit I would have worn it. I arrived precisely on time at his office in the Rolex building on Fifth Avenue. Alan greeted me at the door. I was terrified. He was dressed casually and was waving an unlit cigar. We went into his office and talked for a long time — about the script, comedy, tennis, and food. He took a few calls while I was there, from his wife, a friend or two, his wife again. I studied his expressions, his body language, and his voice. I couldn't wait to start filming this guy. He was absolutely perfect.

Joel arranged for Alan to fly out to Los Angeles and shoot a promotional photo display, the kind you see standing in theater lobbies, which would show the studio how terrific he'd look in the part. They spent an entire day shooting stills, with Alan going in and out of makeup and wardrobe for different looks. To this day, I don't know who paid for it.

When the display was finished being produced, I flew out to Los Angeles to pitch the movie one more time. We invited the studio heads into a conference room where the "standee" had been placed. It was impressive. Alan, pictured in full commando gear, about nine feet tall and brandishing an automatic weapon, was bursting through a wall on which four different posters from the previous "Killer Charlie" movies had been pasted. Every one of them had a totally different action-movie look, and in each, Alan had a slightly different hairline.

The movie never got made. The studio was afraid to spend so much money on my directing debut, especially without a big-time movie star in the lead. What idiots!

Joel went on to produce many movies and pretty much reinvented the action-comedy genre seen in his *48 Hours*, *Lethal Weapon*, and *Die Hard* series. Alan continued to do the odd film part here and there, playing rabbis and hoodlums, businessmen and fathers-in-law. I never did take a directing job after that, finding enough acting jobs to keep me busy.

Every once in a while, I dig out the *Killer Charlie V* script and look through it. It's terribly dated now but still has some enjoyable sequences. I like to think that had I directed Alan King in that role, things would have changed for both of us. We'd have had many more wonderful conversations about tennis and food, I might have continued directing once in a while, and most important, new audiences would have seen what a terrific actor Alan was.

I've always believed that comedians make the best actors. Just look at Jackie Gleason in *The Hustler.* But if you really want to see what I mean, get hold of a copy of Sidney Lumet's 1980 movie *Just Tell Me What You Want.* It has one of the most colorful acting performances I've ever seen.

By a comedian named Alan King.

<hr>

Life According to Alan King

Barbara Walters

Barbara Walters, longtime coanchor of ABC-TV's *20/20* and winner of several Emmy Awards, is most famous for her *Barbara Walters Specials,* in which she interviews celebrities, politicians, and other newsworthy individuals.

I had known Alan nearly all my life. Back in the days of great nightclubs in New York and live performances (were there any other kind?) my father, Lou Walters, owned perhaps the most successful nightclub of them all: the Latin Quarter. So I was then Lou Walters's daughter, a Broadway baby.

And often when the shows were over I would go with my parents to the most famous delicatessen at that time, Lindy's. And there, in the small hours of the morning, having just finished their own shows, the comedians would gather to kibitz and have a corned beef sandwich and swap jokes.

I can hear them now: Joey Adams, Red Buttons, Henny Youngman ("Take my wife, please!"), and Milton Berle pretending to get a shock from his microphone, backing up and saying, "I just got goosed by Westinghouse!" And then there were the young comedians: Jerry Lewis, Buddy Hackett, Jack Carter — and a fresh-faced original named Alan King. With two glasses of wine I could probably do most of Buddy Hackett's act, talking about Jews not being able to ski, but the thing about Alan that set him apart was that you couldn't do his act. Because Alan King didn't tell "jokes," and his performances changed as his life changed. You see, Alan was essentially a philosopher.

He looked at life and what was going on

around him, and that's what he talked about. In the early days, he told stories about his father and his nonexistent brothers, and then, when he got married, there were all those complaints, none of them true, about Jeanette and the kids and bar mitzvahs presided over by rabbis named Chuck. And of course, as the rabbi pointed out, who can forget his gripe at the airlines? Everything ghastly that could happen on an airline happened to Alan, and we recognized every word because it was so true. It was true and it was hilarious.

In recent years, Alan began to talk about the problem of growing old: of surgery on one knee, of arthritis in the other knee, of hair growing out of his ears but not on his head, and of coming to services here at Riverside on Mondays just to see if he had missed anything over the weekend. Alan translated the stages of life for all of us, its pathos and its absurdity. But the man offstage was, if anything, more interesting than the man onstage. Alan was deeply, passionately interested in politics.

Bobby and Ethel Kennedy called him a close friend, and you would just as likely see a presidential candidate in his house as a William Morris agent — more likely, as a matter of fact, unless it was Lou Weiss. And about Alan and Jeanette's house in Kings Point and the water and those beautiful sailboats — I remember him plopping a puppy into my daughter's hands when she was about three, 'cause Alan did love little kids. And we had laughs and hospitality. It was wonderful. Alan had the same friends for fifty years and the same wife. The same beautiful, amazing woman. Jeanette was Alan's best friend, best audience, biggest supporter, best mother to the children. Alan's deepest love. Jeanette and Alan, Alan and Jeanette — they're almost one word. I'm happy for a lot of things for you, Jeanette, and for Alan, not just the children and those adorable grandchildren.

I wish you could see them. No wonder you love them so. But I'm also happy that in the last years Alan also had the recognition for being the superb actor that he was. Alan onstage as Sam Goldwyn, just a few blocks from here — everybody came to see him, and Jeanette would sit backstage and glow as, night after night, audiences gave him standing ovations. Those are great memories to have.

We, each of us here, have our own memories of Alan. Yes, he was sometimes impossible. He was too opinionated, he was stubborn, he talked too much, he talked too loud sometimes, but, man, you could not help but love him because he gave so much back. And now we all have to embrace all the more Alan's partner through life whom we love, now we have to take care of you, Jeanette, the way he would have wanted us to — and we will. I won't go on much longer, Alan, because I don't want you thinking, *Enough already, bring on the cancan girls,* but boy, I wish I could really hear what you think of heaven.

Wouldn't that be something?

And, Alan, if you get a chance, would you give my dad a hug for me?

Alan King Eulogy

Billy Crystal

Billy Crystal is an award-winning actor, writer, comedian, producer, and film director. His TV credits include *Saturday Night Live* and *Soap*; his movie credits include *The Princess Bride*, *When Harry Met Sally*, *City Slickers*, *Analyze This*, and the animated movie *Monsters, Inc.* In addition to his acting credits, he has written and hosted the Academy Awards eight times.

I'm at home and the phone rings. I pick it up and say, "Hello." It's Alan on the other end, and he doesn't. He just starts: "Two Jews are sitting on a bench, one goes 'Oy,' the other goes, 'I thought we weren't going to talk about the kids.' " He waits the appropriate amount of time for him to do a take, and he hangs up. He'd call back, about a week later, and just say, "How's everybody? How you doing? You okay, kid? I love you, you know."

When Jeanette called me on Thursday to tell me this was happening, I sat down at the computer and I wrote "Alan King Eulogy" and it didn't make any sense to me. I kept mistyping — it kept coming out "Alan *Kind* Eulogy." Who was more alive than Alan? Who lived life with more joy than him? He didn't just *live* life, he *devoured* it. He was a well-dressed lion, I once told him. He didn't just enter a room; he *commanded* it.

The first time I ever saw him, I was nine years old. It was at a restaurant in Long Beach; he came in with Jeanette, in a beautiful three-piece suit. I'd seen him on *Ed Sullivan* and when he walked in, everybody applauded him; he turned to everybody and said, "If you love me that much, pick up my check." When I first *met* him, he was producing *The Howard Cosell Show* on Saturday nights and I reminded him of this story, and he said, "Oh, yeah, Russo's, Park Avenue — good food."

Onstage, all energy, perfect blend of humor and hostility. Perfectionist — timing like a Swiss watch. He was a terminator onstage. He would prowl it, push the audience around like they weighed nothing. A champion. Offstage, I found him exactly the same. A perfectionist — rough, tough — but with a sweetness, a caring side that those who were close to him felt all the time. I've called two people "Pop" in my life — my father and Alan.

I loved working with him. I've worked with a lot of people, many of them contemporaries, but Alan was the most fun. We played father and son in the movie. We'd walk on the set together and he'd yell, "Look at us . . . before and after." Early-morning makeup sessions were unforgettable. I'd be sitting in the chair, early, seven-thirty in the morning, laboring over my lines — character, character, character — and he'd walk in and describe in perfect detail what he had eaten the night before. There was never a man who was happier that it was porcini mushroom season. And then the name-dropping — how could anyone have known so many people? He had to be three hundred years old. And I could never top him. I have some good names I can drop too, but I could never top him, and it drove me crazy.

One night we were shooting late on Hollywood Boulevard, right in front of the Chinese Theater — it was perfect for Alan — three, four o'clock in the morning, the crew was sort of bonding — we're sitting right in the middle of the street, no traffic, nothing, and some of the crew were comparing notes on their experiences with drugs in the '60s. I had him. Before I could tell the story of getting my cat stoned on a marijuana brownie and watching him walk backward, Alan, who had been sitting quietly, suddenly just blurted out, "I smoked pot once. It was with Mrs. Lou Gehrig, Buddy Rich, Bishop Sheen, Lana Turner, and two of the Mills brothers." Everybody shut up — we just stared at him. He got up. "I'm going to get a coffee, anybody want anything?" and he left. I couldn't top him. I didn't even get my story about the cat out.

We were very devoted friends. He knew how I felt about him and he made sure to tell me that he respected me as well. He sent the best telegrams, he wrote the best letters, and it was Alan who gave me the best advice before I hosted the Oscars for the first time. He called me up and said, "Listen, kid, put your shoes and socks on first, then your pants." "Why would I do this?" "This way you don't break the crease." I hosted the show eight times — I have eight telegrams that say simply, "Nice crease."

We loved being friends with Alan and Jeanette. I would always tell her, after realizing that there was no oxygen left in the room after a dinner with him, that she is the strongest woman in the world. I had known him only a short amount of time at that point, but I was exhausted from him, but she had done this every day for a lifetime. She once said to me that she thought a tuxedo was pajamas because she would always find him passed out in bed in them.

And now she will have to be strong because this is not going to be easy without him. He loved her and his kids and grandchildren with the same energy that he prowled the stage with. He didn't do anything small. He was big. He was a big noise. He loved big, he lived big, he laughed big. So now what are we going to do? A redwood has fallen in the forest. Who will hold court at the U.S. Open? Who's going to tend to the roses? Who will roam the Friars and make everybody feel good? I learned so much from him. He was a *great* comedian, because he was smart, he was tough, he was honorable, he worked harder than anybody, and he had class. He had dignity and he had a conscience on-stage. He said, "Custard pies doesn't interest me. It's got to have a little bit of intellect in it, otherwise I don't care."

He produced, he interviewed, he acted, he hosted, he was a great businessman, and through it all he was a great husband and father — and he was our friend. And I won't be getting any more phone calls, but I will hear them, and there won't be any more telegrams, but I will get them, and I will read them, and there won't be any more performances, but we will all laugh and we will remember you, Pop.

After a performance I'd seen I'd always tell him, "God, you were good." He'd say, "Ah, I got lucky."

We were the lucky ones. We were the lucky ones.

About the Author

Alan King conceived and developed this book in the period before he died, in May 2004. It would be his final accomplishment in a lifetime of prolific achievement. King was a comedian, actor, producer, author, philanthropist, fashion entrepreneur, pro tennis tournament organizer, chairman of the board, and political activist.

As an author, King had five successful books to his credit, among them his autobiography, *Name-Dropping: The Life and Lies of Alan King*; as well as *Anyone Who Owns His Own Home Deserves It*; *Help! I'm a Prisoner in a Chinese Bakery*; and *Is Salami and Eggs Better Than Sex?* As a performer, King appeared more than one thousand times on virtually every variety show in the annals of TV.

His philanthropic contributions extended to Jerusalem, where he founded the Alan King Diagnostic Medical Center, a thirteen-story hospital complex. He also established a nonsectarian scholarship fund for American students at the Hebrew University and an Albert Einstein Scholarship Fund.

King closely followed politics and civil

rights issues, was always the champion of the maligned and oppressed, campaigned for John and Robert Kennedy, and marched with Martin Luther King Jr.

Most important to him was his marriage of fifty-seven years to his wife, Jeanette, his three children, and six grandchildren.